POPE FRANCIS

POPE FRANCIS

Tradition in Transition

MASSIMO FAGGIOLI

Paulist Press
New York / Mahwah, NJ

Cover image by Rex Features via AP Images
Cover design by Dawn Massa, Lightly Salted Graphics
Book design by Lynn Else

Originally published in Italian as *Papa Francesco e la "Chiesa-Mondo"*
© 2013 Armando Armando s.r.l.
Viale Trastevere, 236 - 00153 Roma
Direzione - Uffi cio Stampa 06/5894525
Direzione editoriale e Redazione 06/5817245
Amministrazione - Uffi cio Abbonamenti 06/5806420

English edition published by Paulist Press
Translation by Sean O'Neill
Copyright © 2015 by Paulist Press, Inc.

Library of Congress Cataloging-in-Publication Data

Faggioli, Massimo.
    [Papa Francesco e la 'chiesa-mondo.' English]
    Pope Francis, tradition in transition / Massimo Faggioli.
        pages cm
    Includes bibliographical references.
    ISBN 978-0-8091-4892-9 (pbk. : alk. paper) — ISBN 9781587684159 (ebook)
    1. Francis, Pope, 1936- 2. Catholic Church—History—21st century. I. Title. II. Title: Tradition in transition.
    BX1378.7.F3413 2015
    282.092—dc23

                                                                                    2014035645

ISBN 978-0-8091-4892-9 (paperback)
ISBN 978-1-58768-415-9 (e-book)

Published by Paulist Press
997 Macarthur Boulevard
Mahwah, New Jersey 07430

www.paulistpress.com

Printed and bound in the
United States of America

CONTENTS

EDITOR'S NOTE

Some of the ideas developed in this book come from writings published during the years 2013 and 2014. For this volume they have been updated in several places and have had their structure reformulated, especially those found in "Da Benedetto XVI a papa Francesco," in *Rassegna di Teologia* (2013/3), pp. 341–64, and "Papa Francesco e la chiesa del concilio," in *Il Mulino* (3/2013), pp. 487–95.

PREFACE

*T*here are various kinds of risks involved in writing about a pope at the beginning of his pontificate, not least of which is the risk of writing a book that is overtaken by events. This is even truer for the pontificate of Pope Francis, who, right from the outset, has given us many surprises that suggest the beginning of a revolution in the Catholic Church. This is one of the reasons why, after the election of Pope Francis, many observers of the Roman pontificate reacted with a sort of stunned silence: some because the new pope's first steps were a shock in terms of their expectations of a peaceful transition, others because of the primary need to listen and understand what was happening.

This book is a clear violation of the order of silence, which must be justified in some way. One initial reason is the moment in history that the Church experienced in 2013, including the surprise resignation of Pope Benedict XVI announced on February 11, 2013, and the conclave of March and beyond, right up to the beginning of Pope Francis's pontificate on March 13, 2013: the extraordinary circumstances require the effort of understanding a series of events that says a lot about the situation of the Catholic Church, but also a more general crisis of how authority is "represented" in the Western world. A second reason is linked to the legacy of Pope Francis and the problem of expectations: the task of reviving the Roman Catholic Church from a crisis of credibility and authority has certainly raised the expectations of observers, but also the expectations of those who have the task of explaining what is going on right now in the Catholic Church. From this point of view, the challenge for those who interpret Pope Francis is infinitely smaller than the challenge that the pope has facing him, but the two challenges are related to each other.

This is not, of course, a biography of Pope Francis, nor is it a complete chronicle of the early months of his pontificate. It is, rather, an attempt to capture some special moments and some key issues at the heart of the transition from Pope Benedict XVI to Francis, with the intuition that this unexpected transition—how it is carried out, and what it has given rise to—reveals something that is not only a special "Catholic event," but also a particular historical moment in a tradition in flux: a tradition that touches the contemporary world far beyond the borders of Rome and Roman Catholicism.

This book is the result of a year of conferences, talks, reflections, and observations: partly originating from the American academic environment in which I carry out my teaching and research, but largely from other opportunities, which are equally fascinating and challenging. Among the opportunities for which I am grateful is the proposal, by the publisher Armando in Rome and by the editor-at-large Enrico Iacometti, that these considerations be put in writing, now that we have some distance from the conclave. They are the result of a series of meetings held in various places in 2013 in the United States and Canada, Italy, England, Spain, and Indonesia.

Among those with whom I have had the pleasure of sharing these occasions and who made them possible, I would like to thank Stefano Baldolini; John Baldovin, SJ; Chris Bellitto; Giorgio Bernardelli; Enzo Bianchi; Lino Breda and all the friends of the community of Bose; Lorenzo Biondi; Hans Christoffersen; Kathleen Cummings; E. J. Dionne, Jr.; Giovanni Ferrò; Richard Gaillardetz; Enrico Galavotti; Paolo Gamberini, SJ; David Gibson; Tom Heneghan; Michael Hollerich; Peter Hünermann; Cathleen

Kaveny; Francesca Lozito; Gerard Mannion; James Martin, SJ; Mark Massa, SJ; James McCartin; Alberto Melloni; Antonio Menniti Ippolito; Robert Mickens; Javier Oñate Landa; John O'Malley, SJ; Marcello Mattè; Marcello Neri and the friends of *Il Regno* and of the Dehoniani in Bologna; Serena Noceti; Heru Prakosa, SJ; Federico Ruozzi; Silvia Scatena; Chiara Scesa; Gerald Schlabach; David Schultenover, SJ; Katarina Schuth; Bruno Simili; Piero Stefani; Maureen Sullivan, OP; Miriam Turrini; Andrea Vicini, SJ; Robin Young; Andrea Zerbini; and the friends of the *loggette* in Camaldoli.

Finally, my heartfelt thank you goes to my friends at Paulist Press: Chris Bellitto, Mark-David Janus, and Bob Byrns for coming up with the idea of an English translation of this book.

The dedication goes to Francesco, Francesca C., Francesco C., and Francesco S., with thanks.

PROLOGUE

Tradition in Transition:
The Resignation of Benedict XVI

THE PETRINE MINISTRY AND THE
"MYSTIQUE OF THE PAPACY"

*T*he resignation of Pope Benedict XVI was an unprecedented event in the history of the modern global papacy: it is not clear whether this resignation has ushered in a precedent, in contrast to the resignation that took place in medieval times and in a wholly different situation. It is certain, however, that the resignation of Benedict XVI has marked a shift in the form of the pope's power in the Church and in the idea of the papacy inside and outside the Church.

The ongoing redefinition of the "mystique of the papacy" as the widespread perception of the pope's power is consistent with the long-term ecclesiological trajectories of Vatican II, but other aspects are still unknown. Looking at the biblical roots of ministry in the church, the "mystique of the papacy" is also rooted in the fact that the papal ministry is a fusion of the prophetic tradition, the priestly office, and the kingly imperial Roman mission. After the loss of the Papal States in 1870, the papacy then lost another typical element of monarchs—that they die in office. In recent times, the popes have been seen not only as priests but also as leader-prophets of the Church—especially in the age of "relativism," in which counterculturalism seems to be one of the typical tasks of the Church in the post-Constantinian period. But the act of resignation seems to change the prophetic aspect of the papal ministry: it seems to make it transferable, or changeable through the prophetic gesture of retiring to a life of prayer.

As we know, canon 332 of the Code of Canon Law provides for the possibility of the pope's resignation: in this case, the Church has shown that it is not a totalitarian system in which the pope is a sovereign acting in a "state of emergency." The formula used by Benedict XVI to explain the decision—"*Ingravescentem aetatem*, advanced age"[1]—recalls word for word the title of Pope Paul VI's *motu proprio*, *Ingravescentem Aetatem*, which, in 1970, introduced the age limit of 75 years for the cardinals of the Roman Curia (and of 80 years for those entering the conclave for the election of a new pope), after which a document of the Second Vatican Council in 1965 introduced the age limit for diocesan bishops.[2]

There is a personal interpretation of these resignations. Observers would have been less surprised by the resignation of Benedict XVI from his pontificate in the early years, especially between 2006 and early 2010, his most difficult years, which were punctuated by the diplomatic incidents of the Regensburg speech, the case of the anti-Semitic Lefebvrian Bishop Williamson,[3] and the reverberations of the sexual abuse scandals in America and Europe, which made Benedict XVI a prime target (in some cases, even in the law courts).[4]

But there is also a functional interpretation of his resignation, which in a sense is testimony to the conciliar experience of Joseph Ratzinger. The Second Vatican Council was the beginning of the redefinition of the "professional profile" for all ministers of the church, but especially for the Catholic bishops throughout the whole world: a job that became more and more complex, requiring the skills typical of a leader, a mediator, an expert media communicator, and a CEO—but always subject to the Vatican and with a mandate that ends at age seventy-five for bishops.[5] From now on, in the theology of the papacy and canonical science, some might say that the law of the Church on the resignation of bishops also applies to the pope, the bishop of Rome. But at the time of the resignation, in the month of February 2013, many questions remained open. Questions about the conclave, or what the pope's role would be in it and in its preparation, about the future of Joseph Ratzinger—who was already Benedict XVI, the first pope emeritus—about Ratzinger's agenda and whether it would remain valid for the conclave of 2013 and for the future pope.

From the theological, spiritual, and ideological point of view, the resignation suddenly left several Catholics "orphans" in the Roman curia, among the bishops, among theologians, and among neoconservatives, especially in Italy and the United States. Pope Benedict XVI's act of resignation has reshaped the Roman papacy, in a way only a pope, and certainly not an ecumenical council or synod, could do. In fact, Pope Benedict acted *"ex sese, non autem ex consensu Ecclesiae,"* as stated in *Pastor Aeternus*, the Constitution on the Church from the First Vatican Council (1870). This act made by the pope should be seen not only in the context of the troubled history of the papacy of Benedict XVI, but also in the context of a lengthy historical period. The history of the papacy is one of creation and then decay, and of shelving many of the theological-political titles used to describe and make effective the power of the bishop of Rome in the Church and in the world—long before these two were not only separate, but also distinct. Gregory VII (1073–85) introduces the definition of the Roman Church as *omnium ecclesiarum mater*: the Church of Rome is not only the center and the link, but it is the "mother," the source and origin of all the churches. With *Dictatus Papae* (1075), Gregory VII establishes virtually no limit to papal authority. The transition from *vicarius Petri to vicarius Christi* takes place under Innocent III (1198–1216), but was again perfected by Innocent IV (1243–54), with the description of the pope as *princeps legibus solutus.* Nevertheless, the Roman papacy grows enormously between the medieval age of Christianity and the modern age, reaching a peak in Vatican I and the age of the "Romanization" of Catholicism in the world throughout the "long nineteenth century."[6] This growth has been possible due to not only the definition and delimitation of infallibility and primacy forced on the First Vatican Council by Pope Pius IX, but also due to the concentration of power in the church in Rome, as never before in the government of the Church. All this continued to grow until Vatican II, when we have a first movement that seeks to reduce this inflation of papal power and papal titles.[7] Vatican II opened the "micro-fractures" in the ecclesiology of the papacy and the episcopacy, which made it possible for Benedict XVI to pass the papacy to his successor by resigning.[8]

We are facing a dramatic transition in the tradition of the papacy from one form to another.[9] What happened between February and March 2013 is one of the most recent developments in the reception of Vatican II, the purpose of which was to restore a more traditional (but not traditionalist) balance in Catholic ecclesiology. This meant depriving the pope of some titles and powers that the papal office took on in the second millennium, between Gregory VII and the beginning of the twentieth century. At Vatican II, John XXIII and Paul VI accepted the end of the Papal States and of the temporal power of the pope in 1870 as a sign of divine providence. The pontificate of John Paul II, however, was typical of a father of the Second Vatican Council, but only for *ad extra* matters; for *ad intra* issues, John Paul II was not able to see the office of Peter as something one can resign, and even less as a ministry to be exercised jointly.[10]

Now the resignation of Benedict XVI could introduce the idea of a "mandate," redefining the mystique of the modern papacy, namely the widespread perception of the power of the pope, which is based on a theological tradition no less than on an imaginary audience that touches Catholics and non-Catholics, believers and nonbelievers. The papacy of the third millennium might come to mean something similar to that of the first millennium—something that Prof. Dr. Joseph Ratzinger had said more than once, and already in 1976, almost twenty years before John Paul II in his encyclical *Ut unum sint* (1995) brought the reform of the papacy to the table of ecumenical relations.[11] Or we could be heading toward a new model better suited to serve unity in the kind of Catholicism that is now global.

This act of Benedict XVI's reconfigures the relationship between the papacy and the Roman Curia on the one hand, and Rome, Italy, the *global south*, and the Catholic and non-Catholic Churches on the other. We will see how the reception of this act will be able to interact with some of the legacies of the post–Vatican II, such as, for example, the process of canonizing popes of the twentieth century and the "aura of martyrdom" that surrounds the memory of John Paul II—not because of the assassination attempt, but for the way in which he died as a pope.[12] One of the new elements of the papacy in the twentieth century is, in fact, personal holiness: to be a saint seems to have become not so much a possible consequence of being pope, but first of all, one of the requirements for exercising the Petrine ministry.[13] You may be wondering if this resignation of Benedict XVI could mean a creeping bureaucratization of the papacy, a few years after John Paul II caused people to assume that "the institutional papacy" and "charismatic papacy" are both part of the role of the bishop of Rome—and this happened in the Church of John Paul II, no doubt at the expense of the charisma of all other bishops. On the other hand, if we read this resignation as an act of accepting Vatican II and *Ut unum sint*, it is worth remembering that the Catholic and ecumenical reception of the ecclesiology of the papacy of Vatican II showed the need for a new "institutional humility" for the papacy in an ecumenical context. The resignation makes the papal office less sacred, less charismatic, and more "functional." It remains to be seen whether it also makes it more collegial.[14]

The Bishop of Rome emeritus, Benedict XVI retreats to a convent in the Vatican, and this choice is not only perfectly consistent with the "monastic theology" typical of Joseph Ratzinger, but also a sign of kenosis.

FAREWELL AND THE BEGINNING OF THE CONCLAVE

The last speech by Pope Benedict XVI, held in St. Peter's Square at the last general audience on Wednesday, February 27, was not the most important of the papacy from the theological and public point of view, but it was perhaps the best given by Joseph Ratzinger as a bishop and as a pastor.[15] In a sense, the last audience represented not so much an attempt to shape his legacy and the Church's perception of him, but the realization of an opportunity missed by the successor of John Paul II: the pastoral touch of that farewell speech said a lot, through his deviation from the magisterium's approach of the previous eight years, and Benedict XVI's difficulties in stepping into the role of bishop and pastor. Only time could tell whether Pope Benedict XVI would be a much more "popular" pope emeritus than he was as the reigning pope on the Chair of Peter.

In his speech, the pope made no secret of the difficulties experienced in his pontificate. The speech was not without the overtones typical of the speeches of John XXIII, which were intended to recast the "papal mystique"—the aura of sacredness around the papacy over the centuries, created not only as an office in the church, but also around the person. Although in some ways Pope Benedict XVI's pontificate should be read in cultural and theological continuity with that of John Paul II, his speech of February 27 instead reinforced the diversity between them: primarily for his ability to depersonalize the papacy, or rather, to live it in a personal way without imprisoning him in a mystical athleticism that did not fit in Joseph Ratzinger. In a way that is typical of the "institutional humility" that is part of the theology of the papacy from Vatican II onward, Benedict XVI emphasized the pastoral dimension of the ministry:

> But I also receive many many letters from ordinary people who write to me simply and from the heart, and who show me their affection, an affection born of our being together with Christ Jesus, in the Church. These people do not write to me in the way one writes, for example, to a prince or some important person whom they do not know. They write to me as brothers and sisters, as sons and daughters, with a sense of a very affectionate family bond. Here one can sense palpably what the Church is—not an organization, an association for religious or humanitarian ends, but a living body, a communion of brothers and sisters in the Body of Christ, which makes us all one.

Dying in public, as John Paul II did, or admitting in public the difficulty, even for Pope Benedict XVI, of giving up any "privacy" (a term that enters the vocabulary of a Roman pontiff, for the first time, in reference to himself): "because he no longer belongs to himself, he belongs to all." These are two different ways, both of which are countercultural, of witnessing to the Christian message to the world of today. At that extraordinary stage of the sacred in the West that is the square of St. Peter's in Rome, the pope took leave of the public, but not from the Church.

The resignation of Benedict XVI, which became effective a few hours later, at eight o'clock in the evening of February 28, 2013, opened a new era in the history of the contemporary church and the papacy, because from many points of view it opened up a gap. The most immediately visible gap was in juridical-canonical and liturgical symbolism. From the point of view of the management of the central government of the Church, it also ushered in an unprecedented situation: the existence together of two popes, the pope who was newly elected by the conclave of 2013, and the pope who had just resigned, Pope Benedict XVI. Beyond the issues of the "logistics of the pope emeritus," there are issues that are less visible but no less critical. The Roman pontificate, in fact, has evolved in recent decades toward a spiritual ministry, but maintains strong and visible elements of power in the Church: some of that are codified; some that are impossible to legislate and codify. Among the elements that are not coded because they cannot be codified is the fact that every pope of the modern age creates a following, which is much more important than what can be accounted for by Twitter followers. The pope today, thanks to the means of mass communication, has a media following and a spiritual following, made up of theological heirs, ideological admirers, and adherents within the power system of the Roman Curia. Each of these followers (consciously or not) must choose between loyalty to the person of Joseph Ratzinger, "Bishop emeritus of Rome," and loyalty to the new pope. In another time, there would have been the risk of a schism within Catholicism, between obedience to Benedict XVI and obedience to the newly elected pope.[16]

In the history of the papacy, one of the most delicate issues concerns dealing with the memory of the departed pontiff. The "institutional memory" that the church has of a late Pontiff is not the opposite, but the companion of "institutional amnesia"—the need for institutions and communities to forget some aspects of their past, in order to maintain cohesion and heal wounds. After the resignation of Benedict XVI, the Church should seek a balance between memory and amnesia that is much more complex than usual: historical judgment on his papacy remains open, more open than it was for the global charismatic pontificate of John Paul II. To make a judgment on Pope emeritus Benedict XVI, who is still alive but retired, if not reclusive, will be even more difficult than it was for John Paul II immediately after his death. But it is undeniable that the historical judgment on Benedict XVI cannot be bound to the judgment on the reign of his predecessor, John Paul II, of whom the theologian Joseph Ratzinger was the main theological reference point in terms of the political doctrine of the papacy for over a quarter of a century. In 2006, Alberto Melloni predicted that the pontificate of Benedict XVI would be a "reign of settling" after the twenty-seven-year-long tenure of Pope John Paul II.[17] If this is true, then the resignation of Benedict XVI shed light not only on the personality and the theology of Joseph Ratzinger, but also on the legacy of John Paul II. In that sense, February 28, 2013, assumes the value of a break point, because with the resignation of Benedict XVI, the thrust of John Paul II's pontificate was depleted in a more traumatic way than on April 2, 2005.

For this reason, the agenda of the conclave of 2013, and of Francis's pontificate "in coexistence" with the pope emeritus, can be read in the light of the challenges raised by John Paul II: challenges that Benedict XVI tried to take up, by forcing the issue in some cases (the challenge of secularism, the distrust of political mediation) and by eliminating others, which were typical of Pope John Paul II (the relationship between Christianity and non-European cultures, the "theology of the body" and the "feminine genius"). After February 28, 2013, the Roman pontificate was set to reformulate itself in a more radical way than John XXIII and Paul VI, the popes of Vatican II, had already done: the relationship with the Curia, with Rome, with Italy, with the "global south"; the papacy as a function of time or as personal charisma; the papacy and the unity of an increasingly fragmented Church; the theologian pope or the pope of government. All these issues (and others, such as those of sexuality and the role of women in the church, which had already been raised at the Synod of 1999 by Cardinal Martini) were dealt with under the wide mantle of John Paul II.[18]

CHAPTER ONE
THE 2013 CONCLAVE
AND THE ELECTION
OF POPE FRANCIS

A CONCLAVE DECIDED BY THOSE
ON THE MARGINS: *URBS ET ORBIS*

*T*he conclave of March 2013 had quite unusual character-istics for different reasons, primarily due to the presence of the outgoing pope, who was still alive and who chose not to have any role in the conclave, if not in its preparation.[1] But other factors made the conclave that elected Jorge Maria Bergoglio on the fifth ballot on March 13, 2013, an event that had the potential to mark a turning point for the Catholic Church. In particular, some facts emerged as a surprise with regard to what was expected.

First, the conclave in 2013 seems to have finally returned the Catholic Church to its global dimension and scaled back Italy's aspirations for the papacy. In this sense, the conclave has restored to the Catholic Church an image of itself that is much closer to that of Vatican II than it has been in recent years: the Church was realigned, from *urbs* to the *orbis*, in a more "world Church" dimension, just as it was in that council—according to the most important theologian of Vatican II, Yves Congar—"*orbis* had almost taken possession of *urbs*."[2] In the days before the conclave, many saw Italy resurface and, due to a consistent set of votes in the hands of Italian and curial cardinals, aspire to the papacy again thirty-five years after the election of the last Italian pope, John Paul I, in the shape of Angelo Scola, Cardinal Archbishop of Milan. But the Italian factor in the 2013 conclave was dealing with a formidable handicap: the diminished international role of Italy, which went hand in hand with the diminished international role of the Italian church.

The pressure of international public opinion on the church as a consequence of the scandal of sexual abuse by clergy had also given rise to fears that an "inquisitor" pope would be elected on a platform of "law and order." In this sense, in the pre-conclave climate, the U.S. church and its cardinals played a particularly important role in Rome, and they presented themselves to the press in a particularly active and effective way. Although on the one hand the shadow of scandal still looms over the American church, on the other hand, the American cardinals (especially the Capuchin, Sean O'Malley, from Boston) could provide credentials regarding their ability to manage the consequences of the scandals and not just from the standpoint of legal and public opinion, but also in its pastoral aspects. For the first time in history the prospect of a pope from the United States seemed possible, even though not probable. On the other hand, the pressure of the media, especially on the question of the relationship between the new pope and the sexual abuse scandals, was witnessed by the statement by the Secretary of State on February 23, followed two days later by the announcement of the resignation of the Scottish Cardinal Keith O'Brien and then by his exclusion from the conclave.[3]

A second element of novelty in the days immediately preceding the conclave, was the *motu proprio Notas Nonnullas*, with which Benedict XVI legislated on the conclave (for the second time in the course of his pontificate, after the *motu proprio De aliquibus mutationibus in normis de electione Romani Pontificis* of June 11, 2007) and which gave the cardinals the opportunity to meet prior to the limit of fifteen days from the beginning of the *sede vacante*.[4] Many observers saw in this decision the desire to anticipate the conclave and put a damper on the pre-conclave debate not only in the media but also in the ecclesial world itself and among the cardinals. This was a further indication of the atmosphere of urgency surrounding the conclave.

A third element was Cardinal Sodano's homily at the Papal Mass for the election, in which the former Secretary of State emphasized the need for reconciliation in the Church—in tones quite different from those of Cardinal Ratzinger in the Mass for the election of the pontiff in 2005: The homily focused on the link between the pope's ministry of mercy and the task of building unity in the Church.[5] A little later in the Sistine Chapel, Maltese Cardinal Prosper Grech (eighty-seven years old and a nonvoter), in giving the last meditation in the Sistine Chapel before the *extra omnes* was announced, referred to the risk of a schism in a polarized Church: "Between ultra-traditionalist and ultra-progressive extremists, between priests who rebel against obedience and those who do not recognize the signs of the times, there is always the danger of minor schisms that not only damage the Church, but go against the will of God: unity at any cost."[6] Both of these presentations revealed a self-reflected image of the church of 2013 that was very different from that of the conclave of 2005: the comparison between the *pro eligendo* homilies by Ratzinger and Sodano and between Cantalamessa's and Grech's meditations in the Sistine Chapel reveal a sense of the "state of the Church" being much more fragile and aware in 2013 than in 2005.[7]

A fourth important element in understanding the direction in which the conclave of 2013 was headed was the presentation to the congregation by Cardinal Bergoglio (which was made public only after his election), in which the Archbishop of Buenos Aires dwelt on the themes of evangelization, the "existential margins," the "danger of self-referentiality for the Church," and "spiritual worldliness":

1. Evangelizing implies apostolic zeal. Evangelizing presupposes that the Church has confidence to come out of itself. The Church is called to step outside itself and go to the margins, not just geographically, but also existentially: the margins of the mystery of sin, of pain, of injustice, of ignorance and lack of faith, of thought, of every form of misery.

2. When the Church does not come out of itself in order to evangelize, it becomes self-referential and then becomes sick (think of the woman in the Gospel who was bent double). Through the passage of time, the evils that affect ecclesiastical institutions have their roots in self-referentiality, in a sort of theological narcissism. In the book of Revelation, Jesus says that he stands at the door and knocks. Clearly, the text refers to the fact that he is outside the door and knocks so that he may enter. But sometimes I think that Jesus is knocking from the inside, asking us to let him out. The self-referential Church claims to hold Jesus Christ within it and will not let him out.

3. When the Church is self-referential, without realizing it, it believes it has the light itself; it stops being the *mysterium lunae* and gives rise to that evil that is so grave, that of spiritual worldliness (according to De Lubac, the worst evil that the Church can incur); living in order to give glory only to each other. Simplistically speaking, there are two images of the Church: the evangelizing Church coming out of itself; that of the *Dei Verbum et religiose audiens fidenter proclamans*, or the worldly Church that lives in itself, by itself, for itself. This should illuminate the possible changes and reforms that need to be implemented for the salvation of souls.

4. Thinking about the next pope: a man who, through the contemplation of Jesus Christ and the worship of Jesus Christ, will help the Church to step outside itself to the existential margins, who will help the Church to be the fruitful mother who lives "in the sweet and comforting joy evangelizing."[8]

The conclave of 2013 chose Bergoglio, who was the other candidate in 2005 when Joseph Ratzinger—Benedict XVI—was elected after four ballots as the natural successor to John Paul II. At the fifth vote of the conclave of 2013, the Catholic Church took "the road not taken" (to quote the poet Robert Frost) in the conclave of 2005: in 2013 the College of Cardinals expressed their choice of pope without worrying about whether it would be perceived as a correction to the vote in the 2005 conclave.

In a church environment seemingly dominated by controversies over the "Roman Curia against the rest of the world," the conclave adopted a different approach, in a way that made the election of Bergoglio—Pope Francis—difficult to label, at the time, as a clear victory of one party over the other. Pope Francis had to deal with a portfolio of unsolved problems in the Church, both in terms of the governance of world Catholicism and in terms of solutions to pastoral problems. Benedict XVI had inherited many problems from John Paul II and had added to them new openings to the traditionalists (especially in liturgical matters, with his leniency toward the anti–Vatican II proponents of "reform of the liturgical reform"). Many expected Pope Francis to lighten the ideological tone that fans of Benedict XVI gave to the doctrine of the Catholic Church. Pope Francis is a "first" for many reasons. He is the first non-European and non-Mediterranean pope since the origins of the institution of the Roman papacy. His coming from Latin America will urge the Church to recalculate the geopolitics of Catholicism and move toward the global south. The fact that he is the first Jesuit pope breaks a taboo, and since the Catholic

Church has other opponents to fight, the Society of Jesus will no longer be seen, as it had been for centuries, as a sect within a sect. He is the first pope who has taken the name Francis, and by choosing that name there is a high probability that the papacy will be faithful to the Gospel message, as was radically witnessed by Francis of Assisi. And he is a pope who is the son of immigrants (Italians, in his case), a real "sign of the times," when millions seek work in countries other than their own.[9]

Francis is from Latin America where the Second Vatican Council was embodied in a radical way in "liberation theology," which was decimated by the political doctrines of Wojtyla and Ratzinger, but that has not been forgotten by the theological tradition of the Church. Bergoglio was not a liberation theologian in its ideal-typical form, but he was part of the church that expressed that thought and theological practice, sharing the political and social analysis of the situation of the poor, if not the language and references of the liberation theologians, who in fact received the news of his election with enthusiasm. Latin American Catholicism is simply unthinkable without the Second Vatican Council (1962–65) and the inculturation of its message that took the form of liberation theology in the years between the conferences of Medellín and Puebla.[10] Pope Francis is a pope of Catholic social doctrine, which many bishops and theologians have forgotten, absorbed as they were after the 1980s, in the idea that speaking of the poor is dangerously close to communism. The allegations about his relationship with the military dictatorship in Argentina recall the difficulty for the Catholic clergy in dealing with oppressive regimes, more in terms of seeking a *modus non moriendi* than a *modus vivendi*: in a sense this is a victory for the old "diplomatic school" of the Vatican, which was humiliated by the mismanagement of the Roman Curia under officials appointed by Pope Benedict XVI. The experiences of the *Ostpolitik* of the Catholic Church toward the Soviet Union and the communist countries of Eastern Europe from 1960 to 1989 are still a useful lesson for the

Church in understanding its past and future challenges (for example, in China and Islamic countries).[11]

From the global point of view, Bergoglio's election to the papacy takes on the significance of a course correction that has been imprinted on the Catholic Church, even from the viewpoint of the geopolitics of Catholicism. The Latin American church, which became the laboratory of the social doctrine of the Church under Pope Paul VI, suffered during the pontificates of John Paul II and Benedict XVI: first in the fight against liberation theology, and then because of the Church's clear Eurocentrism. This neglected part of world Catholicism emerged from the conclave with a Jesuit pope, despite an obvious lack of representation in the College of Cardinals. At the time of the conclave of 2013, 42 percent of the world's Catholics were in Latin America (half a billion out of a total of 1.2 billion), but only 19 of 117 cardinals, compared to 62 from Europe (where 25 percent of all Catholics live today). John Paul II had seen the unity of the continent when he convened the Synod of Bishops for the Americas in 1997, but since then the United States has started to go its own way on the world map. Today the ties of the Catholic churches in the United States with those in Latin America are much more tenuous than before—proof that the geopolitics of the States and that of the churches are never completely independent.

But in light of changes in the religious demography of the American continents, it is still legitimate to speak of a unity between the Americas: within the United States, the Latin American element is growing and is critical to the vitality of Catholicism in North America. On the other hand, although the majority of Hispanics in the United States are Catholic, those of Catholic origin are more secularized than Latino Protestants. The Spanish-speaking roots of the new pope resonate in a particular way across the continent, even north of Mexico. But it is also Pope Francis's biography that makes the pontiff closer to a large number of American Catholics: a pope who is an immigrant's son, like

Pope Francis, understands the challenges of a Catholicism of emigration like that of Latinos in the United States, as it divides families between state boundaries.

If John Paul II was faced with the Berlin Wall, then in the case of Latin American Catholics, Pope Francis is faced with the wall represented by the border between the United States and Mexico, that is, between the United States and the rest of the Americas. The Catholic Church's recapturing of the American continent would be the first step to encompassing a world that is obviously less European than it was a hundred, fifty, or twenty years ago. With a Filipino pope such as Cardinal Luis Antonio Tagle, the Church would have ridden the Asian tiger and brought about the displacement of the world's center of gravity toward the Asia-Pacific region. It could be a salutary delay: to begin again from Latin America is also equivalent to a sort of reward for the humiliations inflicted on Latin American theology in the long Wojtyla-Ratzinger period, and a new way of looking at the Second Vatican Council, without which it is impossible to understand the church in Latin America. Now, with Pope Francis, the Church looks to the south, or rather, looks at the world from the south.

THE FIRST MONTH OF POPE FRANCIS: THE POOR AND THE CALL TO MERCY

Despite the attempts of Catholic traditionalists to deemphasize the theological significance of Pope Benedict's resignation and the importance of the handover in March 2013, the first acts of Pope Francis were marked by a discontinuity of style when compared to the pontificate of Benedict XVI. The announcement of the election and the choice of the name on the evening of March 13 were followed by a short speech by the newly elected pope that emphasized the ministry of the pope as Bishop of

Rome, and asked the people in St. Peter's Square to invoke God's blessing on the new pastor of the church in Rome:

> And now, we take up this journey: Bishop and People. This journey of the Church of Rome which presides in charity over all the Churches. A journey of fraternity, of love, of trust among us. Let us always pray for one another. Let us pray for the whole world, that there may be a great spirit of fraternity. It is my hope for you that this journey of the Church, which we start today, and in which my Cardinal Vicar, here present, will assist me, will be fruitful for the evangelization of this most beautiful city. And now I would like to give the blessing, but first—first I ask a favor of you: before the Bishop blesses his people, I ask you to pray to the Lord that he will bless me: the prayer of the people asking the blessing for their Bishop. Let us make, in silence, this prayer: your prayer over me.[12]

In his homily at the Mass celebrated with the Cardinals on March 14 in the Sistine Chapel, Pope Francis emphasized the element of "movement" in the readings of the day and the importance of this element in the life of the Church: "to walk, to build, to confess."[13] In his meeting with representatives of the media on March 16, Pope Francis gave the authentic interpretation of the name "Francis," the saint of Assisi, and spoke explicitly of a "Church that is poor and is for the poor."

> Right away, thinking of the poor, I thought of Francis of Assisi. Then I thought of all the wars, as the votes were still being counted, till the end. Francis is also the man of peace. That is how the name came into my heart: Francis of Assisi. For me, he is the man of

9

poverty, the man of peace, the man who loves and protects creation.[14]

In his homily for the Mass celebrated in the Church of St. Anne in the Vatican on March 17, Pope Francis emphasized the mercy of God, a theme repeated several times during the first few weeks, "I think we too are the people who, on the one hand want to listen to Jesus, but on the other hand, at times, like to find a stick to beat others with, to condemn others."[15]

At the Mass on March 19, 2013, to mark the beginning of the Petrine ministry (and not the "enthronement," as emphasized by the Holy See), Pope Francis returned to the themes that had already been introduced in the first few days.[16] *Poverty, goodness, tenderness,* and *care* were the word-symbols that emerged from the new pontificate. Pope Francis emphasized the theme of tenderness as a style that is essential to a form of love—care, which is difficult to practice in a world that prizes the individual and competition: "Please, I would like to ask all those who have positions of responsibility in economic, political and social life, and all men and women of goodwill: let us be 'protectors' of creation, protectors of God's plan inscribed in nature, protectors of one another and of the environment. Let us not allow omens of destruction and death to accompany the advance of this world!" Remembering to look after the weakest and most fragile was Franciscan, but above all, it was evangelical, the definition of the power of the pope as service was part of the reconfiguration of the Petrine ministry that Pope Francis had announced in the first few days:

> Let us never forget that authentic power is service, and that the Pope too, when exercising power, must enter ever more fully into that service which has its radiant culmination on the Cross. He must be inspired by the lowly, concrete and faithful service which marked Saint Joseph and, like him, he must open his arms to

protect all of God's people and embrace with tender affection the whole of humanity, especially the poorest, the weakest, the least important, those whom Matthew lists in the final judgment on love: the hungry, the thirsty, the stranger, the naked, the sick and those in prison (cf. Mt 25:31–46). Only those who serve with love are able to protect!

Even from the point of view of liturgical style, the Mass of initiation for the pontificate of Pope Francis sent a series of messages that were unequivocal. It is the Church of Vatican II, whose fiftieth anniversary was being celebrated between 2012 and 2015, a church that harks back, without embarrassment, to the time of a fundamental redefinition of its theology and ecclesiology. In his homily and in his speeches, the newly elected pope mentioned several times his predecessors Benedict XVI and John Paul II. He did not expressly quote the council, but for a Latin American bishop like Bergoglio, Vatican II is an essential and obvious part of the experience of the Church. The kiss of peace between the Ecumenical Patriarch of Constantinople and the bishop of Rome at the beginning of his ministry is unthinkable without Vatican II. The form of celebration for the initiation of Pope Francis itself showed, through the solemnity of a rite that was less than two hours long, the "noble simplicity" mentioned in the conciliar constitution *Sacrosanctum Concilium*, the Vatican II document on the reform of the liturgy (the most important reform of the Church in the last five hundred years), which was the first document approved by the council in December 1963.[17] The liturgical form desired by Pope Francis for the initiation of his pontificate conveys an idea of the church that goes back to the Church called to council by Pope John XXIII, and is a notion of the Church that is faithful to the great Christian tradition, and not to the antimodern idealizations of it. The decision by Pope Francis to canonize John XXIII *ex certa scientia* is relevant to this issue.

POPE FRANCIS

The beginning of Francis's pontificate reopened the discussion on the role of the papacy in ecumenical relations between the churches, and in the relations between religions and society. The presence of the Patriarch of Constantinople, Bartholomew, for the first time in history, at the mass to celebrate the beginning of the ministry of the Bishop of Rome and the presence of representatives of other churches, of Judaism and of Islam, and of other religious communities, and the presence of the whole world in Saint Peter's Square at the same time speak of a Church that must return to the trajectories that were initiated fifty years ago. Almost paradoxically, Benedict XVI, the pope who made "continuity with tradition" one of the mantras of official Roman theology, is succeeded by Pope Francis, who was not afraid to show not only the discontinuity of style with his predecessor, but also the discontinuities that the Catholic Church has carried since Vatican II. It is the Second Vatican Council that reformulated for modern times the ancient idea of a "Church that serves and is poor"—an idea that hardly suits the empty pomp of imperial liturgies, from which Pope Francis has made no secret of wanting to free us. A first direct reference to the council appeared in his address at the meeting of March 20, 2013, with the fraternal delegates from other churches and religions. Pope Francis explicitly recalled John XXIII and the decision to convene the council, and he cited paragraph 4 of the Declaration of the Council on Non-Christian Religions, *Nostra Aetate*, the document that best reveals the prophetic nature of that council, in the light of the "signs of the times." Father Bergoglio had a deep relationship with Argentinian Judaism.[18] It is not by chance that *Nostra Aetate* is the first conciliar document quoted by Pope Francis in the course of his pontificate.[19]

In the light of the homilies and speeches of Pope Francis in the first weeks of his pontificate, two themes emerge clearly as characteristic of the new pope's ministry. The first theme is embodied in a visible and undeniable recentering of the person of the successor to Pope Benedict and of the signals that come from

Rome: from power to service, from the court to the margins. This is not media spin, but simply an attempt to show the consequences of the choice of translating the theological centrality of the Gospel of Jesus Christ into the model of bishop and church. Some elements had already emerged in the early days: his asking the people of the local church of Rome to pray over him; the emphasis on his ministry as "bishop of Rome" rather than as pope; his words on the poverty of the Church and the Church's option for the poor; a more basic lifestyle than that of his predecessors; washing of the feet of an inmate of a juvenile prison (and of two women, one a Muslim, for the first time); the literary genre used in preaching, by the use of autobiographical elements and an exhortatory style rather than defining and definitive; the papal Magisterium as pastoral support, expressed in a homiletic way, with the language of spiritual theology, and in a liturgical context.

In the words of his homily for the Mass of Holy Thursday, Pope Francis further expressed his conception of church and service to the "Gospel of the margins": "When the Gospel we preach touches their daily lives, when it runs down like the oil of Aaron to the edges of reality, when it brings light to moments of extreme darkness, to the 'margins' where people of faith are most exposed to the onslaught of those who want to tear down their faith."[20] The non-European pope urged the Church and in particular the priests and bishops to "go out, then, in order to experience our own anointing, its power, and its redemptive efficacy: to the 'margins' where there is suffering, bloodshed, blindness that longs for sight, and prisoners in thrall to many evil masters." The homily on Holy Thursday revealed a profound understanding of the mechanisms of the Church that go beyond the idea of the ecclesiastical institution as a distributor of the sacraments, or worse, as an agency for issuing moralistic threats. Francis does not believe in "The priest who seldom goes out of himself, who anoints little—I won't say 'not at all' because, thank God, the people take the oil from us anyway." Grace always escapes the control of the Church, a church that does not go to the margins offers a model of ministry that results in "sad priests—in some sense becoming collectors of antiques or novelties, instead of being shepherds living with 'the odor of the sheep.'"

The second theme that emerged repeatedly in his homilies of the first week was that of mercy, which was also reflected in his homily as he took possession of St. John Lateran, on April 7, 2013:[21] "In my own life, I have so often seen God's merciful countenance, his patience; I have also seen so many people find the courage to enter the wounds of Jesus by saying to him: Lord, I am here, accept my poverty, hide my sin in your wounds, wash it away with your blood. And I have always seen that God did just this—he accepted them, consoled them, cleansed them, loved them." "The Gospel of the margins" and the "God of mercy" became the corollary to the "new evangelization" launched by Benedict XVI. The conclave of 2013 had realized the gravity of the moment, and the first steps of Pope Francis were a response to the crisis at the beginning of the twenty-first century. If Pope Benedict made clear the contours of the "politics" of the message and its audience (both outside and inside the Church), a "social Catholic" like Pope Francis re-proposed the essence of a theology that is indigestible to the neoliberal economic culture, to a progressivism that finds it hard to accept the ethical demands of Catholic morality as an integral part of the idea of the "common good," and to a gentrified Catholicism that would like to make Jesus Christ a self-righteous moralist. From a certain point of view, the pope who came from the south of the world took note of the marginality and peripheral situation of Christianity in the contemporary world in order to make it not a lamentation on the deplorable state of the Church today, but a key to the pontificate: a Church that starts from the margins.[22]

But the key to the new pontificate is not only the spiritual and theological impetus to a new evangelization, which starts from an idea of the Church as poor and merciful. Pope Francis also gave very strong indications—on April 13, 2013, exactly one month after his election—by announcing that he would set up a committee of eight cardinals (two Europeans, three from the Americas, and one each from Africa, Asia, and Australia—only one of which was from the Roman Curia) as the consultation board for the pope in the government of the Church and the reform of the central government, and to update John Paul II's Apostolic Constitution *Pastor Bonus* (1988).[23] This choice—presented by the pope as the resumption of a "suggestion that emerged during the general congregations prior to the conclave"—is a move toward innovation. Any reforms raised by the pope go to a special commission *above* the Roman Curia, which does not involve the Secretary of State, and whose members were nominated using both geographical and also ecclesiological criteria (some of the members were the presidents of the continental episcopal conferences). From the historical point of view, this committee is very close to the idea already expressed by the Second Vatican Council between 1963 and 1965 of the need for a permanent "board of bishops" surrounding the pope above the Roman Curia—an idea that was absorbed and ultimately scuttled by the creation of the Synod of Bishops by Pope Paul VI in his *motu proprio Apostolica Sollicitudo* on September 15, 1965.[24]

The change of pace from Pope Francis had little to do with the simplistic notion of a "humble pope," just as John XXIII was much more than "a good pope."[25] From the theological point of view, it is one step in the slow acceptance by the ecclesiastical institution of an ecclesiology, which came to maturity in the twentieth century, that emphasizes that the church serves the Gospel much better if its ministers put on Jesus Christ, the "marginal Jew" on the margins of Second Temple Judaism, rather than the Emperor Charlemagne who civilized medieval Europe. From the point of view of personal style, this change of pace requires abandoning the symbols of power, which Pope Francis demonstrated in the first weeks. But from the ecclesiological point of view, the challenge is even greater, because it involves a shift in the Church from the center to the margins: in dealing with politics, economics, and culture—and especially in the Church's relationship to itself. The Church lives in a world in which it is assumed that, through the Internet, everyone is now at the center, online, linked up, free, and in control of themselves. This is, in fact, not the case, and the Catholic Church, thanks to its global outreach, knows this perhaps better than anyone.

Pope Francis comes before us as the pope of *rapprochement*, "reconciliation by proximity," and the appeal to unity in the Church and of the Church in the world, with an interpretation of the message of the Second Vatican Council that is more implicit than explicit, but also is completely unmistakable and irreducible. John Paul II was the last conciliar pope, and Benedict XVI the last pope to participate in Vatican II as a theological consultant. Pope Francis (ordained a priest in 1969, after the end of the council) will take the Church forward with respect to the memory of the council, and for this reason must manage a legacy that is not that simple: during the pontificate of Benedict XVI, the subject of "Vatican II" was again the cause of controversy, so that it came to characterize the Vatican's doctrinal policy in the Ratzinger period, far beyond the intentions of Pope Benedict XVI. The way in which Pope Francis "speaks" of the council with his episcopal style is also indicative of his approach to the entire previous pontificate and the magisterial legacy of Pope Benedict XVI. Pope Francis sees in the Second Vatican Council one of the conditions of the contemporary Church's existence, without the need for fine hermeneutic distinctions in favor of a conservative base that was part of the Ratzinger "party"—and which now finds itself bereft of a pope who had offered to a small minority within Catholicism, who were reluctant to accept the council, a subtle interpretation that is acceptable only to a nonideological audience.

Pope Francis is not the liberal pope that some naïvely expected, nor is he the "non-theologian of liberation" that some proclaimed triumphantly a few minutes after his election. The meeting of Pope Francis with Gustavo Gutierrez on September 12, 2013, and the public rehabilitation of liberation theology in the pages of *L'Osservatore Romano* by the prefect of the Congregation for the Doctrine of the Faith represented a moment of public conversion for the teaching of the Church that embarrassed many of the persecutors of postconciliar Latin-American theology.[26] Francis is also the first pope who sent a message to an official meeting of the "base ecclesial communities" (XIII interecclesial meeting, Brazil, January 7–11, 2014), thus acknowledging these ecclesial Catholic communities, a reality that comes not only from the legacy of Vatican II in Latin America but also from the Church of liberation theology. There is no doubt that Pope Francis represents a U-turn with respect to the ideology of anticonciliar restoration, which is current in some well-established quarters in the western Catholic Church: the theological, liturgical, ecumenical, and interreligious heritage of Vatican II is fully part of the actions and words of Pope Francis.

There is no doubt that Pope Francis has learned from history, and first and foremost from his own personal history, as evidenced by the autobiographical passages of the extraordinary interview with the director of *Civiltà Cattolica*, Antonio Spadaro, published on September 19, 2013, in several languages:

> In my experience as superior in the Society, to be honest, I have not always behaved in that way—that is, I did not always do the necessary consultation. And this was not a good thing. My style of government as a Jesuit at the beginning had many faults. That was a difficult time for the Society: an entire generation of Jesuits had disappeared. Because of this I found myself provincial when I was still very young. I was only 36 years old. That was crazy. I had to deal with difficult situations, and I made my decisions abruptly and by myself. Yes,

but I must add one thing: when I entrust something to someone, I totally trust that person. He or she must make a really big mistake before I rebuke that person. But despite this, eventually people get tired of authoritarianism. My authoritarian and quick manner of making decisions led me to have serious problems and to be accused of being ultraconservative. I lived a time of great interior crisis when I was in Cordova.[27]

A Jesuit provincial, who was uncomfortable within the mechanisms of the Society of Jesus, later became archbishop of a city like Buenos Aires—he changed thanks to his pastoral work with the poor.[28] In the eyes of many of his confreres, it is ironic that, in a sense, Bergoglio became a Jesuit only when he became a bishop—ironic if you think of the teachings of Ignatius of Loyola, founder of the Jesuits, against the idea that the members of the new order could make a career in the Church. But it also says a lot about the ability of this Church of the late twentieth century to change and publicly learn from its mistakes: and the change from Bergoglio to Francis could be just one step toward the further development of this Latin American Jesuit priest. Bergoglio is a bishop of Vatican II in the sense of having a career devoid of "ecclesiological adulteries" (as some council fathers at Vatican II called them) that tend to stain the reputations of many bishops who change from one diocese to another in a very bureaucratic career system that is hardly theologically inspired: only two dioceses appear in the episcopal career of Pope Francis, Buenos Aires and Rome. Also for this reason the term *bishop and people* has a significance in Bergoglio's case that it cannot have for many other bishops and cardinals. There are liberal "dissenting Catholics" who are disappointed by Pope Francis; but there are many more people who notice a change in emphasis in the attitude of the new pope to the key ideas of Vatican II. His pontificate could play a crucial role in removing the past decade's ideological interpretations of Vatican II as liberal or progressive theology, or as a theology that is now outdated and unable to cope with the challenges of the present time. For Catholic theology, Vatican II is the common ground for diverse cultural and political sensitivities, common ground that resists sectarianism and revisionism: it is no coincidence that it is a non-European and non-North American pope who has inherited this task. But there are issues that cannot be solved only through a new "style of Church": the pontificate of Pope Francis will test the strength of conciliar theology to meet the new challenges of the Church, in celebration of fifty years since Vatican II.

CHAPTER TWO
POPE FRANCIS AND THE TRAJECTORIES OF VATICAN II

*T*he unexpected resignation of Pope Benedict XVI ushered in a new phase in the history of the modern papacy. In addition to the need to elect a new pope and the unprecedented coexistence between the pope and the "emeritus bishop of Rome," the long-term consequences of the resignation are not yet clear in terms of redefining the power of the pope within the church and the governance structure of a Catholicism that is by now largely non-European and very global, much more of a "movement" than an "institution" compared to fifty or a hundred years ago. The election of the Argentinian Jesuit Cardinal Bergoglio, who chose the name Francis (which signaled his agenda like none other before), on March 13, 2013, therefore represents a new beginning for the Church, with a pope who looks to the rest of the world with different eyes than those of an Italian, Polish, or German pope.

But the resignation of Benedict XVI and the election of his competitor in the conclave of 2005 also represent a reckoning and a testing for a church that is facing an obvious crisis. European Catholicism is in crisis not only with regard to vocations, but also attendance to sacramental duties, with no significant signs of recovery (every Sunday, many more Asian Catholics go to Mass than European Catholics) and its public role is diminishing. North American Catholicism, which has yet to recover from the institutional devastation and public perception caused by the scandal of sexual abuse by clergy,[1] is split between theological-political cultures and different social-ethnic memberships, so much so that we can talk about different Catholicisms, even if there is no actual segregation between them. In Latin America, the faithful are trickling away from the Catholic Church and choosing Pentecostal and Evangelical churches, despite the attempts at evangelization of some Catholic communities. A similar dynamic occurs in Africa, where there is competition between the various Christian denominations, as well as the confrontation between Christianity and Islam especially around the latitude of the "tenth parallel."[2] All of these challenges are related to the legacy regarding the Roman pontificate that came out of the Second Vatican Council, the event that redefined Catholicism in the modern world.

THE CONCILIAR CHURCH AFTER BENEDICT XVI

Pope Benedict XVI's pontificate represents a quite unique case in the history of the church, due to the pope's resignation. But even from the point of view of its relationship with Vatican II, the nearly eight years of Pope Benedict represent a case study of very great interest. A first and necessary operation of truth is to clear the field of the simplistic myth of the "anticonciliar" Joseph Ratzinger: a myth that is not only historically inaccurate, but also an undeserved gift to those who, over the past few years, have tried to convey this image for the benefit of their own anti-Vatican II ideology. Vatican II is part of the biography of Pope Benedict XVI, as seen in the lecture to the Roman clergy February 14, 2013:[3] but which Vatican II? The core of the speech was the contrast between "the council experienced by the council fathers, that of faith" and "the council of the media." This contrast between theological council (of bishops, theologians, believers) and sociological council (of the media and the "world" in its metaphysical sense) was connected to the homily on Ash Wednesday of 2013, in which the resigning pope pointed the finger at Christians who want to please "the public" and not the Lord, who seek applause and not the truth: he was referring also to the Roman Curia, just as he did in his homily at the Papal Mass for the election of 2005 that brought him to the papacy.[4] And here we are at the core of Ratzinger's thought: a fundamentally pessimistic Augustinian anthropology, a world view that sees the world and the Church as two forces in opposition, which are irreconcilable except at the cost of the elimination of the "Christian character" of the Church.

What is yet to be analyzed, however, is the interpretative attitude of Joseph Ratzinger with regard to the council documents, as an event in the history of the Church, and in its postconciliar developments. In this sense, some typical moments in his pontificate can be linked to Ratzinger's reading of Vatican II. One of the "conciliar" aspects of Benedict XVI was the refocusing of the idea of being "Church" around the figure of Jesus Christ. At the cost of creating a new form of papal magisterium—through the books published by the pontiff on Jesus (despite the clarifications that came from the pope himself on the non-magisterial standing of those books)—Pope Benedict has attempted to give a new image to Catholicism as a particular form of interpretation of the Gospel in the wake of the patristic tradition. In this respect, it must be said that the relativization made by Pope Benedict XVI regarding the institutional aspects of the Church and the papacy has incurred costs from the point of view of the functioning of the administrative machinery of the Roman Curia. In particular, his appointment of Cardinal Bertone as Secretary of State was more akin to the tradition of "cardinal-nephews," or a figure such as

Cardinal Nicholas Coscia for Benedict XIII (1650–1730, pope 1724–30), than to that of the modern organization of the Roman Curia from the nineteenth century onward.[5]

There are many similarities between Benedict XVI and Benedict XIII in the picture that the eminent historian of the papacy Ludwig von Pastor paints of the devout and humble pope, Orsini: "Being almost a stranger in the world, and without knowledge of men, he entrusted himself, with an almost childlike naïveté, to his favorites, who shamefully deceived him....They cast a serious shadow over the five and a half years of Benedict's pontificate."[6]

But Benedict XVI's underestimation of the governmental aspects corresponded, though not without inconsistencies, to the need of the typical "theologian pope" to return to the source of being Christians, Jesus Christ. From here, we understand the emphasis that was often evident in his pontificate on *Dei Verbum*, the Vatican II constitution on revelation and the Word of God, and the systematic lack of political and institutional vision for Catholicism, both internally and externally.[7]

A second aspect of Pope Benedict's "conciliar theology" was in his ecclesiological vision. Together with a clear emphasis on the baroque aestheticism of the Roman court and its secular liturgies, this has tended to decrease the media prominence of the papacy, compared to the legacy of John Paul II. Even here, it is not without costs in terms of the operation of the curia and of the church in general. But the resignation also bears the imprint of an ecclesiology of the papacy that is faithful to the wording and the conciliar spirit that considers some elements of the Church as relative and mutable. From this point of view, Pope Benedict XVI's pontificate represented only a *pars destruens* regarding the issue of reforming the Church's government, with a culminating act—his resignation—but managing the "institutional" aspect of the Church in such a way as to suggest a disinterest (or inability) on the part of the " theologian pope" to confront the issue.

A third aspect, even more problematic, was the Catholic

Church's dialogue with other churches, other religions, and within the Church. All of these dimensions have been clouded by the shadow of negotiations with the Lefebvrians, especially from 2009 onward, which finally came to nothing, even after extreme concessions made to the schismatic anticonciliar community. Particularly problematic was the decision in 2009 to create a special Ordinariate for Anglicans who wish to "return" to the Catholic Church. The consequences of this act are not yet fully apparent, but it is clear that the Constitution *Anglicanorum Coetibus* is an attempt to interpret the ecumenical spirit of Vatican II, however, not without ambiguities.[8] More generally, the Church of Benedict XVI has tended to strengthen its theological and cultural identity rather than build bridges with other churches and religions.

A fourth aspect that has been typical of the past eight years, but also a legacy of Joseph Ratzinger's quarter century at the Congregation for the Doctrine of the Faith, has been investigations against some theologians, especially theologians and religious women in the United States. In America, this doctrinal policy—led by American Cardinal William Levada as prefect of the Congregation (2005–12)—was clearly interpreted as a showdown between the pope and a part of the church—especially the religious women—which was the most active in presenting itself as the type of Catholicism that was theologically "conciliar" and liberal from the point of view of political orientation. Finally, the relationship between Pope Benedict XVI and the spirit of the council should be seen through the effects of his pontificate and his teachings on the debate about the role of the council in theology and in the Catholic Church. The debate on the relationship between Vatican II and "tradition," raised in Benedict XVI's speech to the Roman Curia on December 22, 2005, did not so much raise a controversy, but rather reopened an existing issue.[9] The debate seemed to have returned to the issue of "continuity/ discontinuity," "letter/spirit," which the Synod of Bishops convened by Pope John Paul II in 1985 had brought to its own theological balance.

The step back that became evident during the pontificate of Ratzinger was indicative not only of a moment of ecclesial life, but also the general difficulty of measuring oneself, on the part of Benedict XVI, against the daily reality of things and against the historical nature of ideas and representations, including theological ones.[10]

The price that the moral and intellectual credibility of Catholicism has paid to the idol of "continuity" is already high. The idea of "history" is by far the most important factor of division within Catholic theology after Vatican II and on Vatican II: in the "continuity/discontinuity" debate there are different conceptions of history. On the one hand, there are those who see in the hermeneutics of "continuity" that Joseph Ratzinger has supported since the eighties (a formula that became less trenchant with the combination of "continuity and reform" in his 2005 speech to the Roman Curia) the only possible hermeneutical option regarding Vatican II: they highlight the need to interpret the council in close continuity with the previous tradition, and in particular with that of the Council of Trent, Vatican I, and the papal magisterium. On the other hand, there are those who see two periods in Catholicism—pre–Vatican II and post–Vatican II—and see in this passage of the decisive elements of discontinuity: Vatican II as a turning point for change, and a source of progress for Catholic theology, a view that accepts the liberal paradigm summarily, without problems and without embarrassment.

The different fronts have always struggled to talk to each other. The new element, in recent years, has been the extreme "continuist" position, which for some fans of Benedict XVI had come to stray over into the Lefebvrian position. In Benedict XVI's speech on December 22, 2005, which began as an attempt to answer two different and opposing extremes, the pope's opinion was that both parties (Lefebvrians and liberal theologians) were guilty of seeing a break in the council, and he came to cultivate and encourage only one of the parties; the traditionalists heard in the pope's speech only an appeal to "continuity" and easily put aside the element of "reform." These neo-traditionalists seem to ignore the fact that the understanding of Christianity as a historical phenomenon is not the fault of Vatican II, nor the interpreters of Vatican II.

The teaching of Pope Benedict XVI on Vatican II will remain as one of the most crucial, but also heaviest, legacies of his pontificate, also because the teaching of Pope Benedict on the council are not limited to statements of interpretation. Especially during the first period of his pontificate, in the eighteen months between the speech in December 2005 to the *motu proprio* on the liturgy on July 7, 2007 (and through the positions taken by the interpretation of *Lumen Gentium* by the Congregation for the Doctrine of the Faith on June 29, 2007), Benedict XVI reminded the Church and especially theologians of the need to enhance the continuity between Vatican II and the previous tradition.[11] However, even if the ecclesiological disputes have directly affected only a narrow circle of specialists, the decision to widen use of the preconciliar Mass instead has touched the body of the Church directly because it questioned the link between "liturgical reform" and Vatican II as a council of reform.[12]

Between 2005 and 2009, with the pope's openness toward some issues close to the heart of the Lefebvrian schismatics, it had become clear that there was a trend toward reopening the hermeneutic debate by a pontiff who questioned what had been taken for granted, especially the methodology used by the international scientific community over at least the last fifteen years, for the historical and theological studies of Vatican II.[13] The consequences of this reverberated even outside of the ecclesial communion. The incident of the Regensburg speech on September 12, 2006, although not intended directly as an interpretation of the council, revealed the parameters of Benedict XVI's interpretation of Vatican II as the relationship of Christianity and the Church with their Greek and European heritage. What became more and more evident, as a side effect of the growing "re-Europeanization" of the Church by Benedict XVI, was how conciliar theology was in danger of becoming an established tradition and a symbol only of non-European and non-Western churches, for whom the Second Vatican Council is more a condition of their existence than a topic of hermeneutic debate.[14]

One of the legacies that the papacy leaves the Church (especially that of the seminaries for the training of the clergy), is the polarity between continuity and discontinuity, a polarity that is often accepted uncritically by theologians who are much less refined than Joseph Ratzinger, who is certainly aware of the complexity of the hermeneutics of the council. One of the risks is that not just the spirit of the council or the event, but also the same letter and the documents of Vatican II are likely to fall under the onslaught of revisionism and desire for restoration that is going on perhaps even more at the periphery than in Rome. The center of gravity of the public debate risked to shift from the theological debate on the Second Vatican Council as a starting point for the renewal and reform of the Church to an "official interpretation" of Vatican II as absolute continuity with the previous tradition. This could result in a rejection of the very idea of the council as the decisive moment, in opposition to a concept of continuity in which "tradition" and "reform" overlap each other in a simplistic way, without ever touching upon the issue of the "Catholic traditionalism" (whether Lefebvrian in name or in fact), that in these eight years of his papacy has attempted to make use of the "theologian Pope."[15]

VATICAN II FROM
BENEDICT XVI TO FRANCIS

The Church's crisis at the end of Benedict XVI's pontificate should be read in its historical context, in celebration of the fiftieth anniversary of the Second Vatican Council, the last moment of real and open consultation in Catholicism in a world that has changed dramatically during this half century, much more and much faster than it changed in the fifty years after the Council of Trent (1545–63), which is the real touchstone of Vatican II.[16] In this sense, Benedict XVI's resignation also acknowledged the impossibility of dealing with the urgent issues of the contemporary Church by having a narrow and precautionary interpretation of Vatican II, as done throughout the pontificate of the "theologian Pope" Ratzinger. Paul VI, the pope of Vatican II and of the early post–Vatican II period, guided the ship of council to port at the cost of significant corrections to the council's project of reform (especially regarding the power of the pope vis-à-vis the power of the council), but nevertheless had acted as a "prince reformer" without giving in to attacks (and not just for obvious autobiographical reasons) against the legitimacy of Vatican II and attacks by a traditionalism that was still isolated in small niches. John Paul II, after the brief interlude of Albino Luciani, was the foremost interpreter of Vatican II during the twenty-seven years of his pontificate, with a distinctly personal-charismatic rather than institutional approach on the subject of church government and the relationship between church and the modern world. This mixture of personalization and the centralization of emotional and "sensory" (rather than theological and intellectual) perception of the contradictions and inconsistencies of Catholicism in the face of the complexity and plurality of contemporary politics gave rise to Wojtyla's doctrinal policy, which was conservative on *ad intra* issues (the role of women in the Church, sexuality, ecclesiology) but progressive on *ad extra* issues, matters on which the "magisterium of gestures" is considerably more eloquent than the magisterium published in official texts (the interreligious meeting in Assisi in 1986, Jerusalem in 2000, and Damascus in 2001). John Paul II interpreted Vatican II in different ways according to the different issues, but always asserting not only the legitimacy of the council (and not only of its documents), but its function as a compass for the contemporary Church.

The change of pontificate from John Paul II and Benedict XVI to Francis is not just a leadership change: the resignation of Benedict and the election of Francis are two eminent acts of interpretation, at the top level of the Church, of a vast and under-the-surface change in the way that the Church interprets Vatican II.

During John Paul II's pontificate, the fundamental way to interpret Vatican II was through a "political-cultural filter" in the approach to Vatican II, that has been very effectively and typically described by Peter Steinfels as four trends consolidated in Catholicism: the council as a tragic mistake leading to limitless heresy (the traditionalist interpretation such as Lefebvrianism), the council as victim of erroneous and biased interpretations (the conservative interpretation), the council as a necessary moment of change, reform, and reconciliation between the Church and the modern world (the interpretation of liberal Catholicism), and the council as a chance for revolution that was betrayed (the radical or ultraliberal interpretation).[17]

Benedict XVI's pontificate intervened in this situation, interpreting the conclave of 2005 as a mandate for continuity with the previous long pontificate (of which he had been the chief theologian, as Cardinal Prefect of the Congregation for the Doctrine of the Faith from 1981 to the death of John Paul II), and then bringing in a number of its elements who were trying to reduce the role of the council in the life and theology of the Church. In his speech on December 22, 2005, the pope had made a distinction between the "hermeneutic of continuity and reform" and the "hermeneutic of discontinuity and rupture."[18] That speech was a direct response to the contributions to the scientific debate, particularly in the historicizing of the council as part of the *History of Vatican II*, published in five volumes by Joseph Alberigo,[19] and a reply to the *Theologisches Kommentar* of Vatican II in five volumes between 2004 and 2005 by the theologian Peter Hünermann from Tübingen (a work that was presented to the pope only a few weeks before his speech to the Roman Curia).[20] This interpretation of the council did not change during the pontificate: in his last speech to the Vatican, as pope, on February 14, 2013, in a lengthy speech, Pope Benedict XVI gave the priests of the diocese of Rome a reading of his experience at Vatican II and the role of the council in the history of the Church for the last fifty years, clearly espousing a conservative interpretation of the council. Benedict once again showed the opposition between two different "Vatican II councils": the "true Vatican II" of the Council Fathers against the "virtual Vatican II" built by the mass media and by intellectuals.

But in the conclusions of my book *Vatican II: The Battle for Meaning* (2012), I framed the different positions on Vatican II around theological "macro-issues": (1) Vatican II as the end or the beginning of the renewal; (2) the intertextual dynamic of the council documents; (3) change and historicity in the Church and in theology.[21] Now, it seems to me that the change of pontificate between Benedict XVI and Pope Francis means also a change of paradigm in the way the Church frames the idea of reform in connection with the different interpretations of Vatican II. Political-ideological interpretations of Vatican II will linger for sure, but the balance has shifted toward a more theological and less ideological debate—partially because the political-ideological framework of interpretations is much more typical of the western hemisphere (Europe and North America) than of the rest of the world.

The space carved out by Benedict XVI between 2005 and 2013 showed the clear intention of questioning Vatican II for the first time in the history of the postconciliar papacy. Benedict XVI took on the task of questioning what was acquired by the historical and theological studies on Vatican II, published by the international scientific community (composed also of the best Catholic scholars) from the eighties onward. On the one hand, Benedict XVI put an end to the "conciliar nominalism" typical of John Paul II: nominalism in the sense of Vatican II used as a cover to give legitimacy to new elements in the life of the Church (such as, for instance, the "new Catholic movements") that did not come from Vatican II.[22] On the other hand, Benedict XVI began to minimize those intuitions of Vatican II that were then developed by Pope John Paul II (e.g., on Judaism, Islam, liturgical inculturation). It is hard to deny that the movement against the liturgical reform of Vatican II is a product of the pontificate of Benedict XVI, but Benedict XVI's legacy of teaching and doctrinal policy on Vatican II is such that it has allowed the idea of the two terms—*continuity* and *discontinuity*—to be mutually exclusive, and the idea that "absolute continuity" is equal to "catholicity" to spread. This legitimized the conservative and traditionalist view of Catholicism that identified the historical and hermeneutic studies of Vatican II with the idea of "rupture" and, through transitive property, leading to a *damnatio* of the council and its historical dimension.

If this is the legacy that Pope Francis has inherited from his predecessor regarding the debate on the Second Vatican Council in the Church today, the new pope's first few weeks have shown a full and unequivocal reception of Vatican II:

- The emphasis on the papacy as a ministry of the Bishop of Rome (with important ecclesiological emphases);
- The identification of the name "Francis" with the hope of a "church that is poor and for the poor";
- The meeting with the representatives of other religions in reference to the conciliar document *Nostra Aetate*;
- The new pope's style of liturgical celebrations, with a rapid disposal of the baroque trappings that came back into fashion during Pope Benedict XVI's reign;
- The first homilies focusing on the theme of mercy and the references to the need to relativize (if not profoundly revise) the institutional aspects of the Catholic Church;
- The need for the Church to go into the "margins" of the world.

Particularly significant for understanding Pope Francis's reading of Vatican II were:

- The appointment (announced exactly one month after his election, on April 13) of a *special committee of eight cardinals* (from all continents, and only two from Europe) for the reform of the Roman Curia: it was an unprecedented step in the history of attempts to reform the central government of the Church as it was created in the late sixteenth century. Pope Francis announced a reform of the Curia using a non-curial body with non-curial members, seeking the advice of prelates who had already served as presidents of the continental episcopal conferences, and postponing (or setting aside, at least for the moment) the main route that is usually used by the new pope in shaping his Curia, or in the appointment of new department heads. The committee of eight cardinals reinstated (consciously or unconsciously) one of the original proposals of Vatican II of creating a "Central Council of Bishops" for the government of the universal church in communion with the pope sitting above the Roman Curia.[23]
- The beginning of the *reform of the Roman Curia*, starting with the new dicastery for Vatican finances (announced February 2014), but more generally with a clear reformist view of the central government of the Catholic Church that we had not seen since Vatican II.
- The *appointment of new cardinals* intended to rebalance the composition of the college that better reflects the demographics of global Catholicism and especially of the southern hemisphere.
- The *preparation of the Synod on the family* of 2014, with a role given to the questionnaires and to other levels of the Church (both local and central)—and the role given to a theologian like Cardinal Walter Kasper.

Pope Francis inaugurated a new phase in the reception of Vatican II. The pontificates of the last seventy years have all been defined (in different measures) by the historical-theological debate in relation to the council: Pius XII's failure to reconvene Vatican I and the pope most cited in the documents of Vatican II; John XXIII, convener of the council; Paul VI, explicitly elected to continue the council, which led him to the conclusion at the cost of significant compromises with some of the aspirations that emerged from the council during the council itself; John Paul I, "second row" council father; John Paul II, the last pope who was a member of Vatican II, a key figure of Vatican II and at the same time "stabilizer" of the council reception; Benedict XVI, one of the most important *periti* of Vatican II and, as pope and cardinal, the most important theological "reviewer" of the council and its interpretations. Pope Francis breaks this line of popes biographically involved in Vatican II for biographical reasons (he was ordained a priest in 1969), but also for the specific heritage of the Church in Latin America. The Argentine Jesuit Bergoglio perceives Vatican II as a matter not to be reinterpreted or restricted, but implemented. Pope Francis's view of Vatican II is obviously incompatible with any version of the antimodernist rejection of the *aggiornamento* of the Catholic Church.

THE LEGACY OF VATICAN II AND BERGOGLIO'S PONTIFICATE

Pope Francis's first steps have been evident in the transfer of the pontificate, which is so exceptional because of the coexistence of his predecessor as "bishop emeritus of Rome" who is still living, and because of the obvious discontinuity between Ratzinger and Bergoglio, not only in terms of style, but also in terms of their vision of the Church and their theological and pastoral priorities. This change of pitch (which has already upset the ideological orphans of Pope Benedict: some have maintained a quiet demeanor, others have reacted in a public way, such as traditionalist pro-Lefebvrian Catholics) has implications not only for the life of the Church and the perception of this pontificate, but also for the clear consequences on the legacy of Pope Benedict XVI and in particular on the mantra of "continuity" as the only possible option for the interpretation of Vatican II. Pope Francis only mentioned Vatican II, in the first weeks of his pontificate, on a few occasions (such as the meeting with the representatives of other religions and the meeting with the Pontifical Biblical Commission) and has carefully avoided interacting directly with the problematic teaching of Ratzinger on the council. But the practical theology personified by the new pope follows directly from the council, as one would expect from a Latin American Jesuit, ordained in 1969: he does not need to invoke or justify the council, since it comes from a time in the history of the church that is an inseparable part of contemporary Catholicism, especially outside of Europe.

The conciliarity of Pope Francis has, however, some unknown factors, such as how Vatican II is to be received and applied throughout the new pontificate. The first kind of uncertainty comes from the issues that most clearly were affected by the interruption of the council's direction—a break that was not started by, but culminated in, the pontificate of Benedict XVI.[24] Interreligious dialogue is one of the cases—if not the main issue—for understanding the relationship between the "letter" and the "spirit" of the council and the necessary "surpluses" of Vatican II with respect to its textual interpretation even on the part of the magisterium—by interpreting texts that were designed, developed, and voted on fifty years ago, in a cultural and spiritual situation that is different from that at the beginning of the twentieth century. If the pontificate of Benedict XVI welcomed *Nostra Aetate*, the Conciliar Declaration on Non-Christian Religions, especially regarding relations with Judaism from the theological point of view, it certainly has reduced the possibility of interpreting it compared to the rest of Vatican II. Another trajectory of the postconciliar church that was interrupted was that of the globalization of Catholicism, not only regarding the internationalization of its executives (Ratzinger had largely re-Italianized the church administration, particularly the Roman Curia and the College of Cardinals), but especially in terms of the ability to "inculturate" Catholicism into cultures other than what exists within Europe, which is now largely in the minority in the demographic balance within world Christianity and especially worldwide Catholicism. Benedict XVI's problematic theological lecture in Regensburg in September 2006 in fact referred more to the relationship between Christianity and non-European cultures than the language chosen by the pope of Rome to speak about Islam. His attitude regarding the dialogue with Judaism had similar fallout due to the concessions made to the schismatic traditionalism of the Lefebvrian Society of Saint Pius X (SSPX).[25] On both these fronts, Pope Francis promises a recovery from that interruption: at the Angelus on August 11, Pope Francis addressed the Muslims, for the conclusion of the month of Ramadan, calling them "brothers"—the second pope after John Paul II to call Muslims brothers.[26]

As for relations with Judaism and the non-Christian religions in Argentina, Fr. Bergoglio was known for his good relations with the Jews of Argentina (which is very important for the history of Judaism and contemporary Zionism). As a Latin American, Pope Francis will not have to deal with the political and cultural costs that weighed on the German pope relating to the memory of the Holocaust and the selective and self-acquitting memory of itself that German Catholicism had (especially in the fifties and sixties) over the "issue of guilt." As for the globalization of Catholicism, a pope who comes from the extreme south of the continent of Latin America has a cultural and geopolitical vision of the world that is very different from that of the Bavarian pope, and is more in tune with the change of perspective coming out of Vatican II, which was not introduced artificially, but was accepted as a historical fact and as a theological requirement. If it is true that Vatican II was driven by clerical elites and intellectuals of European Catholicism, the spiritual and political force of its decisions came from the ability to express an expansion of Catholic theology—accepted *de jure* and not only *de facto*—beyond the historical, linguistic, and cultural borders of the Mediterranean basin.

A second set of problems related to the interpretation of Vatican II is formed by the unending institutional question of Catholicism. On the one hand, there is the crux of the reform of the Roman Curia that Vatican II attempted to deal with, but was prevented from doing so by the same Curia who had organized the council and which, right up to the end of the council (and beyond), had not lost its grip of control over the status quo.[27] This issue required measures aimed not only at reducing the side effects of the reform of the Curia by Pope Paul VI (in particular, the spoils system and the internationalization of the Curia conducted more on the basis of passport color than on competence), but also at taking up again the insights of the council for a more collegial and synodal Church starting from the top down. Pope Francis seems visibly less afraid than his predecessor was of the postconciliar memory and less influenced by the idea that collegiality in the church is equivalent to disorder, bureaucratization, and a weakening of the countercultural character of Catholicism. The second issue among these ongoing questions is the relationship between center and periphery of the church, between Rome and local churches. During the pontificates of John Paul II and Benedict XVI, the Church had lost considerable ground regarding the first postconciliar push for decentralization (as in the case of liturgical reform and the powers of the national episcopal conferences), and there is no doubt that the conclave of 2013 has taken into account the price paid for a centralization of the Church that is completely counterintuitive when compared to the increasing globalization of Catholicism: also because the centralization of recent years took the form of not only a centralization of procedures in Rome (despite the apparent inability of Rome to manage files), but also a Romanization similar to what non-European Catholicism was subjected to in the mid-nineteenth century with the pontificate of Pius IX. Pope Francis has so far shown an intuition about church issues in a way that is free from the official mantras ruling in the last decade. Bergoglio's talks (first to pre-conclave congregations and then in his homily on Holy Thursday) on the "margins" of the world and the responsibility of the Church to come out of itself opens up new scenarios, but harks back to the idea of rapprochement, of the call to unity expressed by Vatican II in its fundamental documents. But the election of Pope Francis brings to the fore the apparent contradiction between a Church that says it wants to be poor, and a Church that still enjoys legal and financial benefits that are a result of medieval Christianity (in Europe), or the link between Catholicism and colonization (in Latin America), or a nondenominational Christian "civil religion" (in the United States). John Paul II and Benedict XVI never even addressed this apparent contradiction, which was in clear continuity with the opacities of Vatican II about the relationship between the Church and the nation state—with a council that asks states and governments to give up their privileges vis-à-vis the Church (especially regarding the role of governments in episcopal appointments), but which does not renounce the privileges of the Church (especially those derived from what had already been agreed upon in previous centuries). Among the many alternatives available to Pope Francis, there is the option to proceed with the painful work of the constitutional disestablishment of Catholicism (as in North America), or to invoke the paradox of a Church that can be *servante et pauvre*—willing to serve and poor[28]—without being subject to the desires of interested donors, and instead is only a shelter for a state that is neutral but protects the "common good."

A third group of questions touches upon the relationship between the Church and Vatican II in particular, because it concerns the role of the council in the life of the Church, today, on issues about which the council has said little or nothing explicitly. The core is composed of various and individual issues, but they are difficult to separate out from one another. One part of this core concerns issues of ethics, particularly sexual morality: in 1968 the encyclical *Humanae Vitae* by Pope Paul VI was meant to end a debate that had been opened by Vatican II, but since then the debate within the Church has not quieted. In addition, it is related to a second issue, that of the role of women in the Church and the ordained ministry in the Church (women's diaconate, women priests, the inclusion of women in the government of the Church). Vatican II has said nothing on this core of issues: the council met fifty years ago and the feminist wave would have reached Catholic culture only a few years later. But in the perception of some relevant parts of world Catholicism these issues—sexuality, women, ministry—are (rightly or wrongly) the first and most important test for judging the "conciliarity" of a pope. This applies especially to the West, or to that part of world Catholicism that is declining demographically, but still retains much of the (economic and cultural) decision-making power in the worldwide Church. It is therefore evident that the relationship between Pope Francis and Vatican II will be measured not only by the use of the conciliar texts in the teaching or decisions made to fully embrace that event, but also by the signals coming from Rome as to the willingness to open the Church on these issues, which would mean a "conciliar process" that could become a "general council" (to which all the bishops of the Catholic Church are invited), or "plenary councils" (on a continental basis), or "synods of bishops" (proper synods, rather than the purely ornamental versions of previous decades).

The best conciliar theology of the last decade has emphasized the issue of "style" as a key to understanding the specificity of the message of Vatican II.[29] Pope Francis has shown, in his first weeks, a conciliar style that is different from that of his predecessors. It remains to be seen what interpretation of Vatican II Pope Francis will choose: the next challenge is to interpret the silence of the council on the issues raised in the Church and in the modern world over the past fifty years.

After the years that Benedict XVI's pontificate spent chasing an impossible agreement with the Lefebvrians, who are always accusing the council of heresy, the beginning of Pope Francis's pontificate has led to what seems to be a final stalemate in negotiations with the ultratraditionalist community founded by Marcel Lefebvre in the 1970s, which has been formally schismatic since 1988. The Lefebvrians' declaration of June 27, 2013, removed any ambiguity about utopian schemes attempted by some of the Curia aimed at healing the schism with an anticonciliar "continuist" and conservative interpretation of Vatican II regarding the theological tradition of the Church: "The cause of the serious errors which are demolishing the Church lies not in a bad interpretation of the conciliar texts—in a 'hermeneutic of rupture' that would oppose a 'hermeneutic of renewal in continuity'—but rather in the texts themselves."[30]

The declaration of the Lefebvrians dismantled the architecture of the famous speech to the Roman Curia on December 22, 2005, by Benedict XVI,[31] the pope who in the past fifty years had conceded the most to Lefebvrians in the hope of reconciliation. Paradoxically, it was the traditionalist community, which was out of communion with the pope because of Vatican II, that made a clear statement on the value of the council, or on the fact that something really happened in the Church fifty years ago. The pontificate of Pope Francis represents an opportunity for a resumption of dialogue not *on* Vatican II, but *from* Vatican II in the life of the Church.

CHAPTER THREE
THE CHURCH AFTER
THE CENTURY OF
ECCLESIOLOGY

*A*lthough there is a legitimate debate on the return of religious attitudes in the form of the "deprivatization of religion" in the world at the beginning of the twenty-first century,[1] what is less discussed is the issue of the "unchurched reform" of contemporary Christianity. The flourishing of Evangelical and Pentecostal "free churches" throughout the world poses a direct question to Catholicism about the plausibility, if not the cultural and institutional sustainability, of what is called *church*. The question is not without its historical ironies, coming, as it did, after the twentieth century, which many called "the century of the church,"[2] and after a council, Vatican II, which has made the theology of the church, or ecclesiology, its focal point.

The process of de-churching begins very far away. From a certain point of view, it began with the Protestant Reformation, and in the Western world, according to some scholars, at the origin not only of the breakup of the visible unity of Christians, but also of secularization[3]—according to a vision of theological modernity that is much less reassuring than what is offered by Charles Taylor in *A Secular Age*.[4] In fact, unlike the versions of Christianity coming out of the Reformation that have converted themselves into a recognizable membership with a profession of faith, without the necessary sociological and cultural visibility (as in the historic churches of the Protestant tradition), or into a vaguely spiritual-therapeutic "culture" without a theology and a tradition (as in Pentecostal and Evangelical megachurches), the "Catholic question" centers round the sustainability of the Church in the face of a growing crisis regarding the authority and credibility of the ecclesiastical institution. The crisis does not derive primarily from the sexual abuse scandal nor from the separation between the teaching and life of the faithful around the issues of sexual morality, but must be seen in the context of a crisis of systems: the crisis of the Church/churches is nothing more than a reflection of the crisis of politics/state in the Western world.[5] As the French Prime Minister Léon Gambetta (1881–82), said, "Anti-clericalism is not suitable for export": links between the destiny of the Catholic Church and that of the West are obvious, especially at a time when the nature of "Western" Catholicism is being redefined.[6]

In this sense, the election of a pope named Francis takes on a significant political meaning well beyond the short-term convenience of party or ecclesial affiliation: it assumes significance as the last court of appeal with regard to a teaching on policy and politics, typical of the *triste époque* (in the words of Andrea Riccardi) we live in. The challenge of Pope Francis regarding the salvageability of the Church also touches on other key figures and other global forces on the world stage. The secular intellectuals and former Jacobins, who are interested enthusiasts in Catholic conservatism as politically expedient and were very active during the pontificate of Pope Benedict, cannot afford to lose interest prematurely in Pope Francis, whom they are tempted to categorize as a "shepherd pope" who has little knowledge of the perils of postmodernity. But the pontificate of Pope Francis, although different from that of his predecessor in its intellectual premise, is not very different concerning the issue of the relationship between church and state in the Western world. The fate of the Church is not entirely separable from that of the political, cultural, and constitutional system founded in the eleventh century when Europe was in the throes of the Investiture Controversy between Pope Gregory VII and Emperor Henry IV.[7]

The growing family of "denominational" churches, which are a legacy of the Protestant Reformation, includes, sociologically, much of the new post-European Christianity. These churches, which are characterized by a very light ecclesiastical and ecclesiological structure, are the alternative and possibly the substitute for the tradition of the "historic or mainline" churches. In this scenario, Catholicism is the exception to those churches that generally have very light connections to a "tradition" in the broad sense; these tend to be evangelistic but without a universalist claim because they adhere to a congregational type of communitarianism or because they are "ethnic" or "national" churches. The Catholicism of Pope Francis appears on the stage of world Christianity as a *unicum* with respect to other Christian churches, whose universalist claims have always been limited, because they are churches that have failed in the challenge of staying on the scene with the same ubiquity as the colonial empires with which they had come. From this point of view, Pope Francis's Latin America has a different story than that of the bond between missions and colonialism in other continents.

But Pope Francis finds himself faced, first, with the issue of *ecclesia semper reformanda*. On May 13, 2013, two months after the election, the 2013 edition of the Pontifical Yearbook was presented to the pope. On page twenty-three, there were two lines with the words "Francis, bishop of Rome," while the other titles, which through 2012 followed the words "bishop of Rome" on the same page, are instead shown on the next page.[8] It was a clear sign of the will of Pope Francis to redefine the papal primacy, in a different way than the redefinition made by Pope Benedict XVI throughout the eight years of his pontificate until the time of the resignation. But the primacy of the pope exists in a regime of limited powers, much different from the absolutism that is often attributed to it. Media coverage of ecclesial events is part of this regime of limitations (further evidence of the impact of mass media on ecclesiology) at which the bishop of Rome participates as pontiff and pope of the universal Church.[9]

THE CHARISMATIC PAPACY AFTER WOJTYLA

Pope Francis's first World Youth Day (WYD) (July 26–28, 2013) in Brazil in a certain sense sanctioned a second beginning of Bergoglio's pontificate. This is the irony of history: it was a mass event, Wojtyla-style, in a place chosen by the pontificate of Benedict XVI well before his unexpected resignation. Given the differences between him and his predecessor (remember the cold reception given to Benedict XVI in Brazil in 2007), what kind of papacy is taking shape here? Is it a return to the "charismatic papacy" of John Paul II,[10] or is it something else?

There is no doubt that Pope Francis is closer to John Paul II than to Benedict XVI, but the size and the form of the World Youth Day 2013 could alter that perspective. WYD is an event that is based on a mass participation of young people from all over the world, together with the pope, and therefore it focuses on the words and gestures of the pope. It is one of the reasons why liberal Catholicism has always viewed these mass demonstrations with suspicion and would like to place WYD meetings on a national or continental basis—which of course the pope could either not attend or, if he did participate, it would be in a wholly different position with respect to the issue of the universality of the event and therefore of his ministry.

But it seems that Pope Francis is aware of the risks of making the papacy excessively charismatic. First, the time and manner of the transition from Benedict XVI to Francis have somehow "vaccinated" Catholicism based on a monarchic ideology of the papacy:

managing, without undue embarrassment, an encyclical like *Lumen Fidei* (June 29, 2013), which was signed by Pope Francis but was obviously mainly the result of the work of Benedict XVI, testifies on the one hand to the precipitous nature of the resignation of Pope Benedict, and on the other hand, to the capacity of the whole Church to accept magisterial documents in the light of a *sensus ecclesiae*, which is more than we are usually granted.

Second, Pope Francis has repeatedly given indications of wanting to be, as Bishop of Rome, only the "signpost" that leads to the true head of the Church, Jesus Christ. From the point of view of the functioning of Catholicism, then, the conclave of 2013 presented to the church an account of the excessive centralization of the government of the Church, not only in bureaucratic management but also regarding the pastoral results coming out of the appointment and career mechanisms aimed at rewarding the inner circle and "yes men." The WYD in Rio, however, has offered other indications for understanding Pope Francis's type of pontificate: continuity with the style created by Pope John Paul II, and continuity with John Paul II also in embracing every culture as "capable of the Gospel" without deluding ourselves that it is possible to bring global Catholicism under the yoke of the European culture of Athens and Rome. Continuity with John Paul II was also seen with respect to a certain "evangelical" liturgical and paraliturgical style: music, dances, performances, and events of various types. This has to do with the young age of the participants at the WYD event, but also with the Church's knowledge that the challenge of global Catholicism is with the postecclesial Christianity of the charismatics and Pentecostal, or with a piety that is less "enlightened" and more "emotional."[11] The heartfelt and popular Catholicism of Pope Francis is not far from the newly minted evangelicalism (in America, a "social evangelicalism" emerging from the disasters of the G. W. Bush era), that combines a strong sense of Christian tradition and a social and political sensitivity in the best sense: a pro-life Christianity that is not content with denouncing the pro-abortion mentality, but includes the pro-life argument in a context of the Christian social doctrine on work, health, and social justice.

WYD 2013 paraded an "evangelical Catholicism" on Copacabana beach, an evangelicalism that is not modeled on the political-ideological characteristics of the United States in the seventies through the nineties, and does not refer, for instance, to the Catholic evangelicalism advocated by neoconservatives such as George Weigel and Michael Novak.[12] It is a *Catholic evangelism*, which has nothing in common with biblical fundamentalism, but rather refers to a spiritual wisdom that is less Calvinist than very compassionate and inclusive. This does not mean a return to the Catholicism of the fifties, far from it. It is enough to read the statements made by the pope on the plane flying back from Brazil to understand that there are far-reaching pastoral innovations on the horizon (on gays, on divorce, and on women in the Church). But this task is not without risks: the pope who comes from Latin America is expanding the boundaries of Catholicism to accommodate the idea of a worldwide Church.

TWO MANDATES FOR POPE FRANCIS

The conclusion of World Youth Day and the pope's extraordinary press conference on the return flight to Rome shed light on the complexity of Bergoglio's pontificate. From Pope Francis's press conference emerged issues on which Bergoglio was acting with an almost explicit mandate from the conclave that elected him: the reform of the Roman Curia and collegiality in the Church, and the transformation of the IOR (the Vatican Bank) (or even its liquidation?), the purging of those in the Church at all levels who handle large amounts of money. On these issues Pope Francis had no difficulty in referring to and explicitly mentioning the consensus among the cardinals before his election: "All I had to do came from the general congregations of cardinals before the conclave," the pope said about the IOR.[13] However, within this range of issues delegated to the pope by the conclave, Bergoglio acted and spoke with a certain open-mindedness: "I think that the Curia has fallen somewhat from the level it once had, in the days of the old curialists…the profile of the old curialist, faithful, doing his work. We need these people." It was a conclusion with which many observers agree, but it certainly did not earn the pope allies within the Curia: the pope ruled on this *etsi Curia non daretur*— as if the Curia did not exist—with the substantial external support that was acquired through the popularity and authoritativeness gained in the first months of his pontificate, but without being able to rely on a clear group of advisers of his own.

Then there were other issues on which Pope Francis seemed to act beyond or without an explicit mandate from the conclave. These issues are related to those on which the world press focuses: homosexuals, the role of women in the Church, the appeal to those who have left the Church in reaction to a certain "Catholicism of exclusion," which became an issue among the church hierarchy in recent years. On these issues, Pope Francis was acting on his own initiative—which is just as it should be for the bishop of Rome. But first reactions could already be seen. Important feminist theologians, especially in the Anglo-Saxon world, reacted negatively to the closed door with respect to the female priesthood; groups who were nostalgic for a form of baroque Catholicism strengthened their campaign of subtle criticism about the "naïveté" of the Argentinian pope, this time on the change of tone about gays in the Church. Pope Francis spoke on these issues by virtue of his pastoral experience, his sense of the Church, and his perception that he has an implicit "mandate" that comes from world Catholicism rather than from the College of Cardinals who elected him.

In this sense, the first year of pontificate established clearly that Pope Francis acted under two different mandates, the mandate of the conclave and a mandate that could inappropriately be called "popular." The two mandates do not necessarily coincide: one of the challenges for Bergoglio is to mediate between these two different thrusts. The WYD in Rio was an announcement of this difficult mediation: "The characteristics of his pontificate are clear, the route is mapped out. From this point of view, Rio has the force of an encyclical. What remains to be understood is whether the whole ecclesiastical hierarchy will follow him, just as the majority of the people of God seems to understand and follow him."[14] But it is a necessarily complicated task, designed to challenge headwinds from both wings of the worldwide Church, the liberal and the conservative, who, on the issue of gays and women in the Church would have liked many more steps forward or maintenance of the official line, respectively.

With the WYD in Rio, the pontificate of Pope Francis got off the ground, as it were, and with it emerged the first visible fault lines within the Church regarding this pontificate. These cracks are not likely to be reabsorbed easily, especially in forms of Catholicism (such as in the United States) that are very polarized on issues of sexual morality and the role of women in the Church—as could be seen in the United States in the early days after the publication of the interview given to the *Civiltà Cattolica* in September 2013.[15] There is no doubt that the papacy is that of a pope who intends to bring several issues to the heart of the Gospel message and the beginning of the pastoral care of souls, rather than the defense of a doctrine disembodied from reality and stuck in a European cultural-historical paradigm.

But it also appears to be a pontificate completely aimed at reconstructing the internal fabric of the Church that is visibly fragmented: the question is whether it will be a pontificate with less energy and fewer resources for attending to the big international political issues. Judging from the fact that the man who has been appointed to the Secretary of State position, Archbishop Parolin, is a man of diplomacy, it seems that Pope Francis has grasped the need to reinvest in the international role of the Holy See; judging from the vigil for peace in Syria on September 7, 2013, it is clear that Francis's pontificate represents a return of the Catholic Church and Vatican diplomacy to the global scene.

THE "ROMAN CATHOLIC CHURCH," BEYOND ROME

The question mark over the recentering of Catholicism on internal matters should not be viewed necessarily as a risk of withdrawing, but as the consequence of a Catholic Church that is faced with the need to redefine its "Roman" component. The scandals of various kinds and the crisis of credibility that the institution has suffered in recent years are nothing but a symptom of an epochal change and the end of the confluence of the Rome of the Caesars with the Rome of Peter, as the confluence of the royal and priestly powers in the person of the pope of Rome.[16] This combination, which is typical of medieval Christianity, has survived in many symbolic and institutional forms, causing the theological shift engendered by Vatican II fifty years ago, and even before that, when the Papal States were ended in 1870. The issue of a Church "reform"—which was one of the explicit mandates Pope Francis received from the conclave—is none other than a variation of the issue surrounding the end of confluence between Caesar and Peter in the papacy; it therefore goes well beyond a program purification, much less cleansing or "policing" the Church.

Vatican II had in mind, albeit not very explicitly, the complexity of the idea of a "reform" of the papacy and the Church, which was already in the process of leaving the idea of medieval Christendom and moving more toward modernity. In Vatican II, the issue of "reform" is very close to the idea of "conversion," and is expressed with the concepts of *renovatio, purificatio, reformatio, instauratio, mutatio, accomodatio, aptatio*, and *evolutio. Renovatio* and *renovare* are the words most frequently[17] used, and are a symptom of the fact that Vatican II sought "reform" both in the structural-institutional and the spiritual sense.

In the postconciliar church, the two dimensions of the reform are separate. The papal magisterium has become more and more credible from the point of view of the commitment to confessing the sins of the "sons of the church" (especially with John Paul II), but it has become increasingly resistant, first of all to the possibility, especially under Benedict XVI, to the need to reform the structures of the Church. In other words, what has been reproduced is the rift between the two qualities that produce reform, which the American Jesuit Avery Dulles had pointed out as sinfulness and historicity, or the sin in/of the Church and history in/of the Church: the first reform requires purification, the second also requires institutional changes.[18] But in this context, the proverbial resistance of ecclesiastical government to reform (at least throughout the second millennium of the history of Catholicism) has received unexpected help in recent years regarding the crisis induced by the historical disciplines (and especially in the historical-religious discipline) from the postmodern paradigm. Forgetfulness of the historicity of Christianity and of the Church has once again favored the status quo, despite the intent of supporters of religious studies as an academic discipline, which is far more secular than a "theological discipline" like church history. The discussion on "Church reform" is a grand narrative, or at least part of a grand narrative that is at least historical, if not theological: once this has been eliminated, the concept of "reform" loses substance, immediately after the concept of "church."

Pope Francis appears in a context in which he must reposition the concept of "church" not only on the world map, but also on the moral map of contemporary consciousness. The scandals of recent years (primarily that of sexual abuse by clergy uncovered from 2002 onward, but also those revealed by "Vatileaks" in 2012) emphasize even more a typical dimension to John Paul II's and Benedict XVI's teaching on the Church, or its sinfulness. The historicity of the Church, at least under Benedict XVI, had not escaped the crisis of meaning that envelops the West, even in the Catholic Church: a loss of the sense of "church history" is part of a more general loss of a sense of history, and comes only a few years after the proclamation by the West on its victory over the communist world, that "history is over."[19]

Pope Francis and his non-European origins overturn this paradigm that is at once geopolitical and cultural, along with other European and Western paradigms that are typical of Catholicism in the northwestern part of the globe, such as the "Tridentine paradigm," which sees the Council of Trent (1545– 63) as the event that defined once and for all the relationship between Catholicism and historicity.[20] The Latin American pope shows that he has an awareness of the relationship between church and historicity, and between history and theology, that clearly comes under the heading of "inculturation" of the Gospel—cultures in the plural: Pope Francis shows that he can do so in a new way, after the postconciliar Church saw inculturation as an attempt to embody Christianity in non-European cultures as had been enunciated by Vatican II and Paul VI, expressed in a performative way (but not in written magisterial form) by John Paul II, and finally substantially negated by Benedict XVI.

The reform of Roman Catholicism, whose theological and cultural shape goes "beyond Rome" and beyond Europe and the West, requires a rethinking of a number of theological and cultural issues, even before the institutional issues. In fact, one can speak of a "Tridentine paradigm" due in large part to the monocultural, or European, character of the Catholic Church between the sixteenth and nineteenth centuries. But for Vatican II it is difficult to speak of a "paradigm" in terms of a mixture of definitions and instructions, and culture. Vatican II lends itself to being inclusive, not so much as a paradigm, but as a "paradigmatic event"[21] in the sense of a new way of doing theology and being a church that includes:

- *ressourcement* as a return to the sources and to the consequent relativization of other Church edicts: "This sacred Council has several aims in view: it desires to impart an ever increasing vigor to the Christian life of the faithful";[22]
- a dynamic interchange between Scripture, tradition, and teaching, and a recovery of the *sensus fidei* as part of the conciliar hermeneutic discussion. The work of dialogue within the Church comes from the Holy Spirit "if the dialogue in the Church is an interpretation of the five criteria sustained by the Spirit: Scripture, tradition, *sensus fidelium*, theological research and teaching";[23]
- inculturation of Catholicism aimed at making it universal: "There are three great epochs in the history of the Church, and the third has just begun and been made manifest thanks to Vatican II: (1) the short period of Judeo-Christianity, and (2) the era of the Church as the church of a particular cultural group, and in particular of Hellenism and Greek civilization and culture, and (3) the period in which the living space of the Church is essentially the whole world";[24]
- detachment from sociocultural models whose ecclesiological transposition is taken for granted for ministerial roles in the church;
- the pastoral nature of the doctrine that rests on the openness of the conciliar body and drives the acceptance of the council, which depends neither on the conciliar body alone, nor on a "spirit" that is detached from that body or uncertain with respect to that body, but that is an act of acceptance that "necessarily takes the form of a conversion."[25]

Vatican II has meant a new awareness of church, a new ecclesiology, a new way of pursuing theology, and especially new individuals and new places for pursuing theology. In this sense, what is clear is the value of the time of the Second Vatican Council not only for the history of the Church, but also for the history and theology of Christianity as "global history" beginning with the theology of women and the role of women in the Church. In this sense the theology of women proves to be a crucial case for the reception of Vatican II, because of its ability to reveal an essential difference between the two most important councils of modern Catholicism (Trent and Vatican II) and the two periods that have been decisive for postconciliar theology and for the Catholic Church in the last five hundred years.[26]

Beyond the issue of women priests and women deacons (on which, after the election of Pope Francis, some Bishops' Conferences have begun to speak after over a decade of silence imposed by Rome), the first non–Euro-Mediterranean pope's overcoming the Tridentine paradigm touches a wide range of issues relating to "practice" rather than "theology": the issue of women in the Church disrupts a number of assumptions that have been taken for granted about the ancillarity of women in the Church, and in particular on the structures for participation in the life of the Church when making decisions on the ministry, on liturgy as a source of inspiration for the regulation of the life of the Church, on the teaching about sexuality and corporeality. From this point of view, Bergoglio's papacy is also a declaration by the Vatican, a truce on the battle front with feminist theology—which lasted throughout the pontificate of Benedict XVI—and with the American nuns of the LCWR: it remains to be seen how this truce (which also applies to other areas of tension between Rome and religious[27]) will be accepted by American theologians.

The truce declared by Bergoglio on this and other fronts involves a reshuffling of entrenched positions within Western Catholicism. In fact, overcoming the Roman Tridentine and

European paradigm has very important implications, not from a "progressive" or "liberal" point of view (which are Euro-Western categories), but from a perspective of theological *ressourcement*, a "return to the sources" that it intends to make the largest church in the world a church that is more faithful to the original message than to the social, political, and cultural aspects of more recent times. Pope Francis showed awareness of the needs of the Eurocentric paradigm through his gestures rather than his words, and of the urgency of this missionary perspective. The Synod on the new evangelization in 2012 had shown more awareness of the issue that clarifies the solutions and perspectives: the election of Pope Francis links the new evangelization to the redefinition of a cultural-theological paradigm in Europe.

If the return to a certain theological Eurocentrism was without doubt one of the characteristics of the pontificate of Benedict XVI, the election of Pope Francis marks the renewal of an attempt to globalize Catholicism, which began with Vatican II. It is no coincidence that the beginning of the pontificate of Pope Francis led, a few weeks later, to the conclusion of the disastrous "negotiations" with the traditionalist schism of the Lefebvrians, who are the standard-bearer of a Catholicism that is more Roman than Catholic, and that after the council, in the schismatic community-based Ecône, he saw this Romanist faction trample the "universal" sense of Catholicism.[28]

REFORMING THE CHURCH, AS WELL AS THE ESTABLISHMENT

The shift in the cultural paradigm that the Catholic Church is faced with cannot take place only at the level of the structure, unless the illusions experienced during the pontificate of John Paul II are to be repeated. The institutional question has been open for a long time in the Catholic Church, but the conclave of

2013, which came after a decade of scandals (the "Vatileaks" scandal more than anything else has led to tangible evidence of the charges that had been known for quite some time) and has accelerated awareness even by those parts of the Church, that is, the college of cardinals and the bishops, who for a long time have not made a truthful contribution in this matter.

It is increasingly clear that from the point of view of the structural reforms of the Church emerging from Second Vatican Council, this is a work in progress:

> As at Vatican I, Vatican II was not able to complete its work. Vatican II has remained a construction site. Beside the old building of Vatican centralization of the nineteenth and twentieth centuries, tower the four massive pillars of a renewed Church and a renewed ecclesiology: the Church as the People of God, the Church as the sacrament of God's kingdom in the world, the College of bishops, and ecumenism. While the building erected by centralization awaits demolition, as happened in due course with the Basilica of St. Peter's, the four supporting pillars of a renewed Church and a renewed ecclesiology wait to be crowned by a dome that draws them towards "unity."[29]

The conclave of 2013 marks fifty years since the last election of a pope who ran the Roman Curia, Pope Paul VI, and on that basis, remodeled it according to the principles of rationalization, standardization, and centralization, acknowledging in a selective manner the message from Vatican II with the apostolic constitution *Regimini Universae Ecclesiae* (August 15, 1967). But regardless of the opinion that one can give of the semi-presidential reform of the Roman Curia and the style of government of Paul VI, there is little doubt that Paul VI was the last pope to govern the Roman Curia, before the "charismatic government" of John

Paul II over the Church and the disastrous "benign neglect" of Benedict XVI toward the Roman Curia. The problems of the institutional issue of the Catholic Church, and in particular the reform of the papacy and of the universal government of the Church, have clearly been open since the pontificate of John Paul II and especially since the Apostolic Constitution *Pastor Bonus* of 1988, which reformed the Roman Curia, and the encyclical *Ut Unum Sint* of 1995 that raised with the Church and indeed with all the churches the issue of how the papacy should be exercised.[30]

The fact that two key pontificates, such as those that governed the Church between 1978 and 2013, were distinguished by the lack of a government of the Church through its bureaucracy, leaves many questions open: on the governance of the universal Church, but also on the type of popes who succeeded one another on the throne of Peter at the beginning of the post–Vatican II Church. Even in this sense, the pontificate of Pope Francis is a test case. But the theological and canonical scholarly consensus on the government of the universal Church is the same as that of the council.[31] From the council until now, no pope has managed to reconcile the papal primacy, episcopal collegiality, and synodality of the whole Church in a way that did not look like a step backward compared to the opening of the council. The issue of the relationship between the center and periphery in the universal Church has become even more urgent, not only for the actual globalization of Catholicism, but also because of the obvious closures that occurred during the long Wojtyla-Ratzinger pontificates from the Code of Canon Law (1983) to the letter of the Congregation for the Doctrine of Faith *Communionis Notio* (1992) and John Paul II's *motu proprio* about the national bishops conferences *Apostolos Suos* (1998).

The monarchical papacy "re-formed" and "re-grouped" itself rather than "being reformed" in the postconciliar years: in opposition to the council, and to a large extent in spite of the council, by acquiring other entities modeled on the Curia itself as a lesser evil compared to other more radical hypotheses (Paul VI's creation of the Synod of Bishops, *Apostolica Sollicitudo*, September 15, 1965), or by accepting it but circumscribing the power of other bodies (such as the national bishops' conferences) that, by now, are absolutely essential for the survival of the Catholic churches in all the nations of every continent. In these first fifty years after the council, Roman papacy has attempted to be "collegial," and after Wojtyla's long period of ambiguity between the personalization of the papacy and collegial ecclesiology, Ratzinger-Benedict XVI had sometimes given the impression of intending to return to the absolutist and anti-collegial model. The resignation of Pope Benedict XVI and its impact on the next conclave reopen the question of the shape of the papacy, which in this last half century has certainly been redefined by its successes (its projection on the global scene) and its failures (the pressure exerted by this global dimension of the papacy on the "margins" of the geographical Church).

But there are other failures that are part of the institutional history of the postconciliar Catholic Church (in addition to the Synod of Bishops), and there are many local and partial successes (such as plenary councils and diocesan synods); and there are successes that have a high risk of being dismantled (such as diocesan and parish pastoral councils). Bergoglio's pontificate assumes, for that matter, the function of an indication of the ability of the Church to reform itself institutionally, thanks to the resources in its outlying parts, because of a man who has never been part of its central government, but played important roles in his local and continental church, first as provincial of the Jesuits, and then as archbishop.

Among the areas for the first postconciliar pope to explore is the eternal question of the institutional Catholic Church. Even from a biographical point of view, the issues include: the intermediate (continental) level, of which Bergoglio has had direct experience as chairman of the drafting committee for the final document of the assembly of Latin American bishops in Aparecida in 2007;[32] the relationship between the territorial church (parishes and dioceses) and the "new Catholic movements";[33] the participation of women and laity in church government (something that is already happening on a daily basis, *extra legem* if not *contra legem* in many countries); and a rethinking of the functions of papal diplomacy.[34] The creation of the "council of eight cardinals" by Pope Francis on April 13, 2013, thus has particular importance: not only for its historical significance, which inaugurates a precedent in the history of the modern Church, but also because, just four weeks from the election to the papacy, it is a formal admission of the existence of an institutional issue.[35]

John XXIII was able to put pressure on the Roman Curia at the beginning of his pontificate by convening the Second Vatican Council. But the question of the institutional Catholic Church has now been open for over half a century. It remains to be seen what way Pope Francis will go, since from the point of view of the general structure, he inherits a Roman Curia that is substantially intact in terms of the reform of Paul VI in the 1967 Apostolic Constitution *Regimini Ecclesiae Universae*. That reform came out of the experience of young Montini in the Roman Curia far more than from the Second Vatican Council: Paul VI had realized in his own way "the dream of Pope Pius XII: a reform of the Curia from the center."[36]

But it is clear that Pope Francis has in mind not only theological and institutional reforms, but spiritual ones. The speeches he made to the Brazilian bishops and to the Latin American Episcopal Council on July 27 and 28, 2013, while traveling in Brazil, tell us a lot. In the first address, the pope spoke of a "grammar of simplicity," of "a Church which accompanies [people] on their journey; a Church able to make sense of the 'night' contained in the flight of so many of our brothers and sisters"; a Church that since Vatican II has been able to become "more mature, open, generous, and missionary."[37] In his second address the pope launched, even more clearly, the "internal renewal of the Church" and "dialogue with the world today" (with a clear reappropriation of *Gaudium et Spes* by the papal magisterium, after the Ratzinger years), denouncing as "temptations" the "ideologization of the Gospel message," "functionalism," and "clericalism":

> Bishops must be pastors, close to people, must be fathers and brothers, and be gentle, patient and merciful. Men who love poverty, both interior poverty, as freedom before the Lord, and exterior poverty, as simplicity and austerity of life. Men who do not think and behave like "princes." Men who are not ambitious, who are married to one Church without having their eyes on another. Men capable of watching over the flock entrusted to them and protecting everything that keeps it together: guarding their people out of concern for the dangers which could threaten them, but above all instilling hope: so that light will shine in people's hearts. Men capable of supporting with love and patience God's dealings with his people. The Bishop has to be among his people in three ways: ahead of them, pointing the way; among them, keeping them together and preventing them from being scattered; and behind them, ensuring that no one is left behind, but also, and primarily, so that the flock itself can find new paths.[38]

The new form of pastoral ministry launched by Bergoglio does not end with institutional reform. But it does have clear institutional implications, as seen from the signs of new collegial practices within the Roman Curia, not only with the appointment of the board of eight cardinals, but also with the extraordinary summit of the Roman Curia convened on September 10, 2013, and the important speech given to the Congregation for the bishops on February 27, 2014, about Francis's *speculum episcopi*—the model of Catholic bishop: in choosing a bishop,

It is always essential to guarantee God's sovereignty. The choice cannot be dictated by our demands, conditioned by possible "stables," factions or hegemonies. Two fundamental realities are needed for guaranteeing this sovereignty: the tribunal of one's own *conscience* before God, and *collegiality*. And this is the guarantee. These two realities are essential from the first steps of our complex work (from the Nunciatures to the work of Officials, Members and Superiors): one's conscience before God and collegial commitment. Not arbitrary power but discernment together. No one can manage everything; each one, with humility and honesty, lays his own badge in a mosaic which belongs to God.[39]

EPILOGUE

A Papacy for the World Church

FRANCIS'S PAPACY AND
THE GLOBAL EMPIRE

*T*he election of Bergoglio to the papacy is an unprecedented step toward the fulfillment of what the German Jesuit theologian Karl Rahner called the "world Church," that is, a third macro-period of its history (after the Judeo-Christianity of its origins, and the church of Hellenism and of Greek-Latin culture) with the self-realization of the Church as a church in the global dimension through the incarnation of Catholicism in different cultures.[1] If the Second Vatican Council was the first council of the world Church, and Pope John XXIII was the first pope of a Church that was conceived as worldwide, then the pontificate of Pope Francis is the first pontificate of a bishop from the world Church. No wonder Pope Francis is redefining the dimensions of the Church, making it "simply practicable again, after it had been taken away from the people who are the Church because of the undue pervasiveness of ecclesiastical power."[2] This not only signals the end of a certain clerical power, but also of the clerical power and of a certain part of the world Church within Catholicism. The extraordinary experience of Church at the Extraordinary Synod celebrated in Rome in October 2014 is evidence of the change Pope Francis is bringing to the Church. Change is happening at many levels, but the first level is in terms of style of Church and style of leadership of the bishop of Rome in a global Church that is now very polycentric and whose demographics is sustained by churches geographically and culturally very distant from the former capital of the Roman Empire.

In fact, there is also a "political" side to the Church that is being redefined, beginning with the redefinition of the papacy. In the history of modern Catholicism, from Vatican I onwards, the Church has seen different types of popes, from the point of view of style: the kingly pope, Pius IX; the diplomat pope, Pius XII; the pastor pope, John XXIII; the reformer pope, Paul VI; the international-star pope, John Paul II; the theologian pope, Benedict XVI. The history of the evolution of the "pope's image" in the last 150 years says a lot more than the theological definitions of the papacy about the relationship between the role of the papacy, the various visions of the Church, and the Church's role in the world.

John XXIII, the last Vatican diplomat to be elected pope (the last in a series that sees Pius XI and Pius XII, his predecessors, eminent diplomats), the pope who calls Vatican II, is the first *global* pope who opens the Church to a global self-understanding. The politics of John XXIII is global in terms of its "claims"—a Church that for the first time advocates universal human rights—but global also in terms of "representation"—representing the "Catholic Church" in the sense "*universal, comprehensive*" character of Catholicism in his experience in Eastern Europe (*geographically*) and in his experience as a Church historian (*chronologically*). Roncalli brought this "universalist" understanding of Catholicism into a world and into a Church divided by the Cold War—a Cold War that since the very beginning of the post-World War II period, had made of Catholicism an ideological pillar of the "free world" in the western hemisphere. Roncalli addresses the issue of the ideological polarization with a vigorous engagement with the protagonists of the Cold War (especially Kennedy and Khruschev in the

Cuban missile crisis), with the beginning of the Vatican *Ostpolitik*. But at the same time Roncalli works at liberating the Catholic Church—globally, in Italy—from a preset ideological alliance with ideological anti-Communism. The two encyclicals that are pillars of his political message are *Mater et Magistra* (May 1961) and *Pacem in Terris* (April 1963).

Paul VI, son of a Christian Democrat politician silenced by Fascism, a Catholic Italian with deep connections with the French-speaking world (like his predecessor Roncalli), brings Vatican II to a conclusion, pushing hard for the approval of the constitution *Gaudium et Spes*—in those same weeks when he (as the first pope in history) addresses the United Nations in New York (October 4, 1965), reformulating the "global claim" of the Catholic Church in the modern world. Paul VI is the pope of a Church programmatically open to dialogue with his first encyclical *Ecclesiam Suam* (August 1964). Montini had been introduced to the idea of America by Jacques Maritain, and Paul VI is the first in a series of three popes with an easy connection with America—if we make an exception for the reception of *Humanae Vitae*. Paul VI advocates a public role of the Church tightly connected to the idea of evangelization as inseparable from the idea of "human development" and an idea of "progress": the encyclical *Populorum Progressio* (March 26, 1967) is probably the most "radical" social-political teaching coming from a pope thus far.

John Paul II inaugurates a new period in the "politics" of the papacy. Wojtyla's election entails the chance to build a strong alliance between the Vatican and the United States against the common enemy, that is, Communist regimes in Soviet Russia and Eastern Europe (but also Cuba and East Asia). In 1984 the beginning of formal diplomatic relations between the Holy See and the United States signaled the changes brought by the Cold War to the relationship between the Catholic Church and international politics. The Polish bishop who, at Vatican II, had been a strong advocate of religious freedom (in the sense of freedom of the Catholic

Church from Communism), becomes the first pope to receive a U.S. Ambassador to the Holy See. After the fall of the Berlin Wall, the politics of John Paul II shows more complexity. On the one side, in the social encyclicals, John Paul II offers a response to the Western illusions of the "end of history" in favor of a definitive victory of capitalistic democracies. On the other side, John Paul II preempts the coming "clash of civilizations" described by Samuel Huntington and works at liberating the national-ideological narratives from the religious-theological discourse—with the visits to Casablanca, in the synagogue of Rome, the first interreligious meeting of Assisi in 1986, up to the visit to the Mosque of Damascus in 2001. All these prophetic insights become part of the Catholic reception of the political-religious catastrophe represented by the attacks of September 11, 2001, and the wars that follow.

Despite all the talk about the continuity between Benedict XVI and John Paul II, Joseph Ratzinger offers quite a different political message during his pontificate. Benedict's encyclicals, especially *Caritas in Veritate*, continue on the line of a strong message of "social justice." But there are a few issues typical of Ratzinger-Benedict. First, Benedict was fundamentally unable to develop the "theology of the nations" of John Paul II: as a German pope, the "German question" lingered for the whole pontificate and became particularly burdensome in some instances, especially in the relations between the Vatican and the Jews and the State of Israel. Second, the conflict with the theology of liberation in the 1980s was translated in his pontificate as a deep distrust of the possibility of the Catholic Church to become involved and engaged in social and political issues without becoming contaminated by them. In this sense, the politics of Benedict is typical of a postmodern culture in which the legitimacy of politics acted within the classical boundaries of the nation-state and the role of the "empire" is heavily questioned by Ratzinger's complex political theology.

Pope Francis inherits this legacy of a very "geo-political" Catholic Church: this is not a recent invention. One of the most fascinating perspectives, and one that is much needed for under-standing the importance of the Catholic Church in the global sce-nario, is that of Catholicism as the heir to the Roman Empire: an empire that the Church has survived and taken over many cen-turies after the beginning of that turbulent but highly successful marriage between the Church and the political power held by emperors Constantine and Theodosius between AD 313 and 380. Another of the theories that is more accredited and more recent describes the Catholic Church as a spiritual, cultural, and politi-cal force that was able, during the pontificate of John Paul II, and with the help of Ronald Reagan, to bring down the Berlin Wall and put an end to the historical experience of communism in Eastern Europe. These two examples speak of a strong attraction-repulsion mechanism in the history of Catholicism and empire. But if they say a lot about the historical dependence of Catholicism on the role of history in the formation of its own cul-tural and political identity, they say little—positive—about the features of the institutional Church as the "ultimate empire." Much less explored is the question of how, in fact, this last global empire has managed to survive as an institution in a social and political context that has seen great change over the last century: from the era of colonial empires to the age of multinational eco-nomic-financial empires; from nationalism to that of the crisis of legitimacy of the nation state in the west; from the world domi-nated by Western powers to a global world increasingly oriented towards the south and east; from the world of the "state religion" to the world of religious freedom and, at the same time, of the *revanche de Dieu* and of the "clash of civilizations."

By now, we have become accustomed to the fascination with which the church of Rome, the papacy, its symbols and its tradi-tions, are looked to by groups that may be numerically limited but are politically and culturally influential in the Western world: those who are nostalgic for the cultural Marxist hegemony over the Western world and its powerful representation of a social moral message; those who go on about the decadence of the west and who appear to be disenchanted, but are very happy about the apparent immutability of the institution of the Church; the survivors of the neoliberal thinking, who took refuge in the arms of a pope like Benedict XVI, who has never made any secret of considering the political culture coming out of the Enlightenment to be the cause of the worst disasters of the modern era; and connoisseurs of political theology and the debate of the twenties and thirties between Carl Schmitt and Erik Peterson. This fascination with Catholicism as the ultimate empire corresponds to a global crisis of leadership in the Western world: the papacy can give the impression that it satisfies the hunger of the west for a way out of this decline that has momentous geopolitical dimensions. But Pope Francis's pontificate comes to alter the cultural and political balance that has been in play for a long time, and that with Benedict XVI seemed to have found its own way of theologizing in spite of the historical evidence.

THE WORLD CHURCH AND GEOPOLITICS

The election of a Latin American pope has significance for the long period of Church history, but also for the geopolitics of Catholicism. He is the first pope, in the contemporary era, to be elected from a country outside Europe, and this also means that he is a pope from an area of the world outside of NATO, or from that alignment of historic Western Catholicism that was one of the characteristic features of grand international politics after the Second World War.[3] From this point of view, 2013 marks the definitive end of a certain type of geopolitical and geo-religious world map, and defined the Cold War, which includes the papacy as well. The recent revival of Russian imperialism in the case of Ukraine at the beginning of 2014 and the pan-Orthodox council of Patriarch of Constantinople Bartholomeos in 2016 are just different elements of a wide range of geopolitical and geo-religious coordinates that are shifting.

At a time when the United States as a global power is investing less and less in Europe in order to turn towards the Asia-Pacific region, the election of Pope Francis raises questions about the relevance of Europe on the map of Catholicism, and consequently on the world map.[4] The demographic decline of European Catholicism has consequences for Europe and for Catholicism: it is a combination that must redefine itself and accept a reduction against the rise of other types of Catholicism, both in terms of its theological and cultural significance, and in the political role played by the European church.

In fact, there are other unknowns that make Pope Francis an object of great interest for understanding the future scenarios of the relationship between Catholicism and world politics. Pope Francis seems much closer to Pope Benedict XVI than to his predecessors of last century, from Pius XI to John Paul II, in terms of a lack of experience in international politics. But Bergoglio's peculiar curriculum, from Jesuit provincial first (1973–79, in opposition to the military dictatorship) and then as archbishop (from 1992, under two popes, John Paul II and Benedict XVI) certainly gave Pope Francis an experience that is hard to match, especially looking at the change in emphasis from Bergoglio the priest (between the periods in which he was provincial of the Jesuits) and that of his tenure as archbishop.[5]

But for a Latin American pope, one of the key issues is the relationship between the papacy and North American Catholicism, especially in the United States. The church in the United States is the energetic face of a Catholicism that is growing, largely thanks to the Latin American immigrant component—a component that has not yet found adequate space inside a church still dominated by European strains and has not been comfortable with the ideological divisions that are typical of a Catholicism that is split in two, reflecting the two-party system in American politics. The election of a Latin American pope affects the way the church in the Americas perceives itself: for the Latin American church, but also for the church in the north of Mexico, which in recent years has weakened many of the ties between the Catholicisms on the two shores of the continent.

The election of Pope Francis represents—in the sense of depicts and shows—a whole new balance in the theological map of Catholicism. Until the Second Vatican Council—the most important church reform since the sixteenth century—it was the European churches and their theological traditions that had the leading role. The churches built by missionaries may have been important participants, but they were not able to build a strong opposition to the Europeans. Not anymore. At the Extraordinary Bishops' Synod of October 2014 on the family, the strongest objections to the German (and some Italian) bishops' proposed welcome to gay and divorced Catholics came from the representatives of English-speaking Catholics from the United States, Africa, and Australia. Their opposition was carefully planned even before the Synod as one can see from the long paper trail of interviews, op-eds, and books laid down by cardinal Raymond Burke (United States) and cardinal George Pell (Australia). Once in Rome, they argued with the Europeans in a way that says a lot about the new sense of self-awareness in their churches back home.

The election of a Latin American Pope, finally, has consequences for European and Italian Catholicism especially, in the sense of the "normality" of their role in relation to a history of being a "special case" and to the aims and ambitions of the papacy as part of the Italian and European political system. The role of the Italian Bishops Conference (CEI), the Italian cardinals and bishops of the Italian church, will redefine itself in the world Church, and with it the weight of Italian politics within the Vatican and the priorities of the pontificate. Italian Catholicism, having passed through several stages—from the dogma of the "political unity of Catholics" to "legitimate pluralism," to

Berlusconi's bipolarization, to the season of the "Todi forum" for a new Catholic "centrism"—is faced with the transition to adulthood. Pope Francis's speech to the CEI on May 23, 2013, allowed us to see the new pontificate's desire to return to the Italian church what belongs to it, and to ask the Italian church how much it can give: "Persevere in brotherhood. May the Italian Episcopal Conference carry ahead this dialogue, as I said, with the cultural, social and political institutions. It is your duty. Go ahead!" The last Italian pope who ruled the Church was Paul VI, who was elected fifty years before Bergoglio, on June 21, 1963: since then the Italian character of the worldwide Church has diminished and its ability to show their indispensability within Catholicism has not predominated. The election of Pope Francis may have finally put to bed Italy's claims not only on the papacy, but also on the Church—thanks to the dramatic loss of credibility of the Roman Curia in these last few years. At this point in history, at least symbolically, Italy seems to have more need of the Church than the Church has of Italy. The Latin American pope paves the way for a return of the Italian church to "normality," which (judging from the first months of Pope Francis) sounds like the opposite of the "normalization" that had free rein in the pontificates of John Paul II and Benedict XVI. This has consequences within the Church, but also within the political field.

In this sense, the conclave in 2013 and the election of Pope Francis also diminish the claims of Italian and European Catholicism to point the way to the world Church, even from the point of view of the cultural and political experience of Catholics. Bergoglio, unlike his predecessors, never had the completely European experience of the rebirth of the continent after the Second World War, thanks to the hegemony of popular Christian-Democratic parties—"the unlikely winner of the post-World War II."[6] As a bishop in Argentina, therefore, Bergoglio has never had to face the problem of the revival of a Catholic political elite, to continue the generation of rebuilders and founders of post-1945

Europe. This also means that Bergoglio did not have to take on some of the characteristic features of the evolution of the political culture of European Catholicism: the marginalization and decline of Catholic organizations of the left, the marginalization of the working class in the Christian Democratic parties in Europe, and the growing liberalization of economic policies implemented by the ruling European Christian Democratic classes. From this point of view, it is clear what kind of Catholic political culture is the source for those who see in Pope Francis's social Catholicism a "radical" or even "populist" platform: from the point of view of the trajectory of the economic and social culture of American neoconservative, and of liberal and free-market Catholicism, there is no doubt that Pope Francis's emphasis on economic and social justice and immigration sounds, to some, subversive.[7]

A completely different relationship there is between the papacy and Communism, for decades one of the poles of the political positioning of Catholicism. For Pope Francis Communism is a wrong ideology, but he often mentions some Communists as good people that he met in his youth. The key role of poverty for Francis's idea of the Church is part of the end of this anti-Communist clause in the political language of the papacy. Talking about the poor does not mean anymore that you are a Communist even if that comes from a Latin American Jesuit.[8] In terms of Vatican global geopolitics, the election of Francis signals a shift towards the south of the world, but also a possible opening to Asia (where Benedict XVI never went): the visit to Korea in August 2014 and the cautious opening coming from the Chinese government are part of this transition to a new "world Church."

But the otherness of Pope Francis regarding European history gives the pontificate a greater freedom than his predecessors, to meet the challenges in relating to other religions on the world map—especially Judaism and Islam—without the baggage of the Church's "European identity," which is an important factor in interfaith dialogue with obvious, not only cultural, but also political and geopolitical, dimensions.

A NEW SYNODAL PROCESS

The new leadership style of Pope Francis is far from being purely a "media-friendly" attitude. It has not only deep theological roots, but also consequences for how the Church—from the bishop of Rome to the rest of the hierarchy and the faithful—interprets the role of the Church in the modern world. Dialogical and synodal leadership style has been associated for too long—especially in the European and Anglo-Saxon quarters of conservative Catholicism—with complacency towards liberal impulses. Until Vatican II, these European and North American Churches were on the "progressive" side of history, in a church still filled with cultural optimism. The church and Christianity were then part of mainstream culture. Then came the sixties, the new legislation on abortion, divorce, and more recently same-sex marriage hit particularly hard some Catholic cultures. The Catholic Church felt pushed to take a countercultural stance. The legacy of the Second Vatican Council became a contested narrative and captive of the "culture wars" of the past thirty years. All this meant, for the leadership culture in the Catholic Church—for popes, bishops, and clergy—taking as much distance as possible for "collegiality," episcopal and otherwise. Pope Francis's different leadership style is part of his new reading of the history of the Church on the last fifty years, and the Synod of 2014 was the first crucial test for his pontificate.

The Bishops' Synod on the family celebrated in the Vatican in October 2014 opened the Saturday evening before on October 4 (feast of St. Francis of Assisi), with a speech by Pope Francis in St. Peter's Square that is in its own right the continuation of the famous "Moonlight speech" of John XXIII of October 1962:

Francis's speech was the "where were we?" of the first truly post-Vatican II pope. Francis talked about collegiality; "the joys and hopes;" Church history as *magistra*, as a teacher; and the blowing wind of Pentecost.[9] This speech was an unequivocal act of reception of the council. Branded by the right-wing Catholics (and sometimes also by left-wingers) as a generational event relevant only for those who were there, Vatican II is still the compass of the Church *in* modernity—a compass that the hierarchy of the Catholic Church seemed to have lost in recent times. Without making reference to Vatican II, it is impossible to recognize the fundamental features of the pastor Jorge Mario Bergoglio as well as of the opposition to this pontificate—both the "constitutional" opposition and the "crypto-Lefebvrist" and ultra-traditionalist opposition. And this is exactly where Pope Francis resumed the conversation, as it is evident if we read the first steps of the pontificate and the first two published documents, the interview with Antonio Spadaro, SJ, editor of *Civiltà Cattolica* (September 19, 2013), and the apostolic exhortation *Evangelii Gaudium* (November 24, 2013).

The Bishop's Synod of October 2014 is a step further in the new reception of Vatican II. Four elements are particularly visible. The first one is the retrieval of the pastoral constitution of Vatican II *Gaudium et Spes*, after a pontificate, like Benedict XVI's, which was marked by a conspicuous distance from the ecclesiology of *Gaudium et Spes*[10] and the attempts to reframe Catholicism in "cultural terms"—after Vatican II's attempt to liberate the Gospel from a particular cultural tradition.

The second point is collegiality and synodality in the Church. Vatican II talks about "episcopal collegiality" (the bishops with the pope), but after Vatican II, it emerged clearly the need of a larger "synodal" dimension (the whole people of God). Pope Francis receives and interprets this, as it is evident from his talking of the Bishops' Synod as an institution of "effective collegiality."[11]

The third point is a renewed vision of Catholic social teaching. At the conclusion of Vatican II, the pastoral constitution

Gaudium et Spes represents at the same time the end of nine-teenth century–early twentieth century Catholic social doctrine and the beginning of a Catholic social doctrine for a modern and pluralistic world, in which the Church is not attached anymore to the prerogatives given by the legacy of European Christendom.[12] Francis talks and quotes *Gaudium et Spes* in unequivocal terms as the beginning of a new chapter in the history of Catholic social teaching.

The fourth point is the pastoral nature of doctrine. Francis's invitation to the bishops to "smell like their sheep" is exactly the opposite of the attempts to undermine Vatican II because it is a "pastoral council"—as opposed to "doctrinal councils" like Trent or Vatican I. The homily of Francis at the inaugural mass of the Synod on October 5, 2014, sounded like the words of the bishops of Rome advocating the cause of the Christian people in the face of the bishops: the pope not only as *defensor civitatis* but also as *defensor populi Christiani*, a pope who speaks on behalf of the people and defies the ecclesiastical establishment.[13]

The Synod of 2014 means also something relevant for the governance of the Catholic Church. The decision of Francis to call a consistory of cardinals for October 20 to discuss the Middle East means the second consistory dedicated to a specific theme within eight months after the consistory of February 20, 2014. The Consistory was one of the collegial institutions of the government of the Church until the early modern period, before it was repealed at the beginning of the seventeenth century. Pope Francis is reviving—along with the national bishops' conferences, the Synod of Bishops, and the new "Council of Nine" cardinals, which he created four weeks after his election as pope—a more collegial style of governing the Catholic Church.

This is part of a bigger plan of Francis for a new synodal Church. What we have seen in those two weeks in October 2014 is something the Church saw already fifty years ago, with a par-ticular kind of interaction between the pope and the bishops gathered to debate: the daily homilies of the pope and the announcement of other meetings decided by the pope (the consistory of October 20). These are messages that the pope sent the assembly: respect of the freedom of the bishops in Synod and contribution to the dynamics of the Synod means for Francis walking a fine line that already Paul VI at Vatican II had to walk.

The experts who studied the history of the Synod of Bishops as an institution designed by the council but created in 1965 by Pope Paul VI (in part also to curb the council's aspiration) know that the Synod of Pope Francis is taking a form similar to that of the original idea of Paul VI. Under John Paul II and Benedict XVI, the Synod was the stage for the celebration of a superficial unanimity of the bishops with the pope. The Synod of Pope Francis is different. There is a clear parallel between the Synod of 2014 and the dynamics of Vatican II. The Synod of 2014 ended on October 19, but that did not end a year of debate in preparation for the Synod in October 2015. Cardinal Marx of Munich made it clear at the Synod that the church needs a public debate on these new issues and it seems that it is not the only one to think so. The same intuition of Pope Francis to celebrate two synods in twelve months on the same theme makes it a natural discussion that does not end in Rome during the weeks of October 2014 and 2015, but is extended in time, in space. In the words of Archbishop Bruno Forte, one of the leaders of the 2014 Synod, the intersession between an assembly and the other may be more important than meeting in Rome—just like at Vatican II.[14]

The Catholic Church is not known for speedy changes, but at certain times this speed changes, and in February 2013 it accelerated dramatically. One of the mantras often repeated by experts said that, given the bishops appointed by John Paul II and Benedict XVI, there was no hope of a resumption of dialogue within the Church, much less the dialogue between the Church and the world. What happened at the Synod instead is evidence that putting people together to debate in a climate of dialogue is much more than the sum of their individuality. Some of the ideas that the bishops and cardinals debated in public so soon after Francis's election would have been prohibited in the church only a couple of years earlier; they were considered so dangerous that bishops thought they would put themselves at risk of dismissal for crimes of opinion. Times have clearly changed: Francis has not changed the times, but he has been able to interpret them.

Despite criticism from conservatives against Pope Francis for allegedly manipulating the assembly, the Synod communicated with great transparency in its most important steps. The pope also decided to publish the final text with the number of votes, paragraph by paragraph. It was a real debate, the first in the history of the modern Synods of the Catholic Church, and the pope came out the winner as one who had believed in the synodal process. Francis is interested in "the beginning of a process" and not to control the outcome—as he said in the exhortation *Evangelii Gaudium* that he published in November 2013.[15]

At the end of the Synod, on October 19, 2014, Francis beatified Pope Paul VI, and in the context of the Catholic Church in 2014, this was an act that said a lot about the direction in which Bergoglio wants to bring Catholicism to the world. It is a return to some intuitions of Paul VI, the Pope who took over the council in the summer of 1963 and brought it to its conclusion and its implementation. This means also a recovery of trajectories that had been partially interrupted during the thirty-five years in the pontificates of Karol Wojtyla and Joseph Ratzinger. The first clear sign of this is the way Pope Francis wanted the Synod of Bishops celebrated, in a really collegial way. But also from the point of view of the theological method, there are similarities between the Synod of Pope Francis and the synods of Paul VI. The 1974 Synod on Evangelization is one of the landmarks of Bergoglio, as we read in the exhortation *Evangelii Gaudium* published in November 2013.

A second indication of the relationship between Francis-Bergoglio and Paul VI-Montini is the vision of the role of the pope in the Church: the real postconciliar reform of the Roman Curia is the one of 1967, not of 1988. Moving the agenda of the reception of the council and the aggiornamento of the church means moving it also from Rome, giving back growing responsibilities of bishops and national bishops' conferences. The obscurity into which Paul VI-Montini had fallen in recent years stemmed from conservatives' hostility to any idea of Church reform and theological development. Paul VI was a "reformer prince,"[16] disliked by radicals because he was a prince and by conservatives because he was a reformer. Francis, whose career in the church before the papacy is exceptional and completely different from that of Paul VI, has a similar view.

The third common element between Paul VI and Pope Francis is a vision of the Church, that is, a deeply conciliar ecclesiology: the documents of Vatican II, especially *Lumen Gentium* (the Church as communion) and *Gaudium et Spes* (the Church in the modern world) and Paul VI's programmatic encyclical *Ecclesiam suam* of 1964 (dialogue as a key word for the Church in the contemporary world) are integral parts of Francis's vocabulary. It is an ecclesiology that is wary of integralisms (both theological and ideological-political), and sees in "mediation" (both in theology as in politics) the necessary condition for the vitality of Christianity in a pluralistic world. Mediation means adaptation, but also inculturation.

Finally, the issue of the encyclical *Humanae Vitae*: many bishops at the 2014 Synod thought it was necessary to revive and rediscover the most famous (and controversial) encyclical on contraception, *Humanae Vitae* of Pope Paul VI, published in 1968. That encyclical was the first major interruption of the dialogue between the Church and modern culture in the postconciliar period: Pope Francis is clearly aware of that. That is why Francis is reframing that encyclical within the conciliar ecclesiology and a friendly relationship between the Church and the world: not only in order to recover Paul VI, but especially to reclaim the Church's credibility when it talks about love, marriage, and human life in a non-ideological way. Francis knows that you can accept what *Humanae Vitae* says about love, marriage, and procreation, and at the same time use contraceptives responsibly and conscientiously in a couple's life. The moral history of the postconciliar Church is also made of these couples of Catholics. Francis is the one who has encountered more than all other popes.

RADICAL, SOCIAL, AND LIBERAL CATHOLICISM: FRANCIS AND AMERICA

All this presents the American Catholic Church with a specific and unique set of challenges. No surprise that the reactions came very soon after the election and even more after the end of the Synod of 2014.[17] But the issue is not only in terms of moral theology about marriage, divorce, and contraception. One of the main changes inaugurated by Pope Francis compared to his immediate predecessors is a different vision on the issue of "politics" for the Catholic Church. It would be easy to identify the diversity of Bergoglio compared to Ratzinger as a lack of "anti-political animus" or as the ability not to be identified with one ideological-political side. But there is a diversity of theological culture that is different than either Wojtyla or Ratzinger that should be emphasized. If the long Wojtyla-Ratzinger pontificate was characterized by the teaching of the Church on moral and social issues, with a strong emphasis on "anthropology" linked to the idea of the "natural law," Pope Francis appears to be motivated by a more historical and cultural vision, in line with the Latin American theology he comes from, and by a more spiritual than theological vision for the ministry of the Roman pontificate. The pontificate of Benedict XVI, "the theologian pope" (in the sense of academic theologian), may be an exception in the history of modern Catholicism.

The shift in emphasis with Bergoglio, from the theological to the spiritual papacy has some unknowns for the future structure of Catholicism. But presenting an alternative to Ratzinger does not make Bergoglio a progressive or a liberal (just as Ratzinger was not a reactionary). Bergoglio is a "social Catholic" with a subtle and complex vision of "modernity," and far more multifaceted than that of the promoters of a simplistic return to an idealized past. In Bergoglio, there is a clear perception of the turn of Western culture towards an individualistic conception of human life, and of the mutation to which the political culture in service of this concept has been subjected. In this sense, it is usually relevant the different nuance of meaning between the word *liberal* in English (in favor of individual freedom, especially in a moral sense and in terms of individual rights) and *liberale* in Italian (in favor of individual economic freedom). But this difference in meaning between *liberal* and *liberale* loses its importance for a social Catholic like Bergoglio.[18]

What is obvious is the novelty brought to the papacy by a Latin American pope: as a Catholic, Bergoglio has never had to take charge of the passage, in the political culture of his Catholicism, from the antidemocratic and antimodern intransigence of the Catholics in the early twentieth century to political, democratic, and constitutional Catholicism in the post-1945 period. In other words, if European Catholics still have the antidemocratic and anticonstitutional (anti-French Revolution) legacy behind them, a Latin American brings with him a different kind of contentiousness with a different and less ideological nature. The issue of democracy, for a Latin America Catholic, is played out not in the context of the French Revolution (and with all the revisionism possible regarding the legacy of Jacobinism), but in the struggle for democracy in Latin America in the grip of the military dictatorships of the late twentieth century.[19]

But there is also another reason why Bergoglio's pontificate emerges as a new element in the discussion on the relationship between Catholicism and the modern world. The internal spasms in the Catholic world in recent years with respect to the role of Vatican II and the years following, with new openness to the modern world—convulsions that have seen the conflict between enthusiasts of Ratzinger on one side and "conciliar Catholics" on the other—derive from a vision of the history of Catholicism in the last fifty years that is completely European, as well as ideological and historically inaccurate. According to this view, we have moved from the idealistically perfect Catholicism of Pius XII, in which the political and cultural scene dominated, to the Second Vatican Council with its encounter with modernity, to the decline of public Catholicism inaugurated in 1968 and sanctioned by the Catholics' compromises with the secular democratic culture. In other words, according to the cliché that is so dear to neoconservative thought, the stability of Catholicism between the 1930s and the 1960s was replaced by a period of historicist, populist, and pauperistic, cultural revolution that would lead to the dissolution of Catholicism as a pillar of the Western world. Bergoglio's pontificate disproves this claim, coming from a Catholic world in which the Second Vatican Council had a totally different effect: the force of the argument presented by the Latin American pope is likely to undermine the solidity of the neoconservative thesis on "Catholicism and modernity" in the late twentieth century from the ecclesial point of view, since it had never been viewed from the historic-scientific perspective.

There is therefore an issue of political and cultural heritage that is part of the election of a South American pope. The fork in the road that appears to have been passed by the election pertains to a re-discussion, not only in light of Vatican II, but also in light of that historical horizon that, for theologians and for the Catholic hierarchy, is part of the debate on the Second Vatican Council, namely 1968, the sixties, and the symbolic break inaugurated by those years. This break is much more pronounced in the consciousness of Europe and North America than in South America and the rest of the world. The election of Bergoglio is part of the relativization of that historical caesura, but also part of the awareness that it is impossible to return to the way the world was before the sixties—unless we want to again "ghettoize" Catholicism culturally, politically, and geographically and make it a refuge from modernity for castaways of various types. The political and ecclesiastical history of the South American continent has its own periodization, which does not view the fifties as a golden age and the sixties as a cultural, political, and moral upheaval that allowed conservatives to view Vatican II as a destabilizing event.

Pope Francis presents new challenges to the world, but also to Catholicism and some of its key elements, particularly in the West. His election took place at a particular historical period in world politics: in 2013, the West was in the sixth or seventh year of an economic crisis that was more severe than that of 1929, and in a cultural context that has seen the poor disappear from the scene—the poor were being overlooked even by the Catholic Church. But Bergoglio had seen up close the catastrophic economic crisis in Argentina, including its financial default in December 2001. The theological-political victory of doctrinal politics in the Vatican over liberation theology had brought with it the elimination of one of the themes of the Second Vatican Council: the poor.[20] In this cultural and ecclesial climate, what emerged particularly strongly was the American Catholic Church's conservative school of the Reagan era, or the U.S. Catholicism that between 1973 (the Supreme Court decision to legalize abortion) and 1980 (the election of Ronald Reagan to the presidency) had moved to a large extent from the Democratic Party (which had been the natural political home of recent Catholic immigrants for almost a century) to the Republican Party. From the late eighties onward, "Catholic Reaganism" also affected the American hierarchy, and gave a decisive boost to the theological formulation of the "culture wars" between the different key elements of American culture, even within Catholicism.[21]

Epilogue

The winning side of political Catholicism in the United States, represented by the conservative and neoconservative strains, chose two pillars for its identity: a pro-life, anti-abortion stance that was isolated from the "social question"; and an economic culture oriented towards free market that was against the public sector and the regulation of the market by politics. In the American "culture wars," two extremes tend to meet: the radical progressive and the conservative, both substantially (but to different extents) oblivious of the great tradition of social Catholicism. With John Paul II and Benedict XVI, it was relatively easy to "Catholicize Americanism" in the shadow of the relentless struggle launched against *liberal* Americanism (feminist theology, a less monarchical church, and especially the abortion, contraception, and homosexuality issues) thanks to the relative leniency towards free-marketer Americanism (in the economy). With Pope Francis, it has become much more difficult for American Catholicism to continue to invoke the magisterium of the pope to perpetuate not only the entrenchment and mutual excommunication between the two major U.S. Catholic cultures (the conservative Republican and the liberal Democratic parties), but also the "exceptional" (in a positive sense) role of the United States on a map of the contemporary world.

In this sense, there is a parallel between John XXIII and Francis: as pope, John tried to disengage Catholicism as such from the Cold War; Francis is trying to disengage Catholicism from the "culture wars." The objections (or worse than objections) against both popes arrive from the ones who see their attempt as an appeasement. There is a clear reversal of trends with Francis, when compared to the pontificates of his two predecessors. This has deep consequences for the relationship between this pontificate and America—if one pays attention to the reactions in some circles of U.S. Catholicism against the apostolic exhortation *Evangelii Gaudium* (November 24, 2013), especially in its section on the economy and social justice.

In other words, what in Italy is the niche of the daily newspaper *Il Foglio*—which tends toward propaganda for a Catholicism that is European, traditionalist, anti-ecumenical, and socially and politically reactionary (like Roberto de Mattei,[22] going back to the theological politics of Charles Maurras)—there are in America, within the vast network of Catholic universities and colleges, circles that are resistant to every attempt to modernize, well-funded think tanks and lobbies that are solidly connected to the episcopate, and politicians who are sincerely convinced of the necessity of a traditionalist Catholicism for the moral health of America, and through this, for Western society. For this reason, the election of Pope Francis is destined to change the dynamics of this internal conflict, especially in North American Catholicism, on policy issues and social justice, which in recent years had seen the magisterium associate itself much more with the neoconservative school than the social. Both sides are faced with a pope who understands the parallels and convergences between these two sides in terms of the privatization and libertarianism of the moral life. The two sides have responded to the election of Bergoglio and to the innovations brought about by him in the first few months each in a different way: if the liberal Catholic culture has embraced the new emphasis of Pope Francis, neoconservative Catholicism reacted with evident coldness, if not confusion, especially in its headquarters in the United States.[23] Not surprisingly, in the environment of American foreign policy and global scenarios, one is dealing with a pope who is likely to "alienate Catholics in the industrialized West who have so far supported the leadership, the doctrine and conservative theology."[24]

It is too early to predict a collision between a "Latin" school of social Catholicism and neoconservative North American evangelical Catholicism. But it is clear that they are two different Catholic cultures within a Western culture in which the idea of self-realization, and "its anthropological narrative, in today's mass narcissism, does not create democracy out of differences, but rather out of obsessive micro-conflict of identity."[25] The novelty is that the neoconservative school (which is certainly no less plagued by conflicts of identity than the liberals) had found open doors in Rome before the election of Francis, and, thanks to this, had been able to present itself as the new generation of Catholics aimed at reconquering modernity.[26] From this point of view, the Catholicism of movement "to the margins" announced by Pope Francis also means trying to take leave of the political culture of neoconservative and neoliberal Catholicism. For neo-orthodox Catholicism (such as the content of publications like *First Things*), the challenge is to find a suitable language for a "faithful dissent," a language that can express disagreement with the teaching in a loyal and faithful way—a language that liberal Catholicism has learned the hard way (although not always adequately) during the pontificates of John Paul II and Benedict XVI. But even within "conciliar" Catholicism in the English-speaking world, the advent of Pope Francis coincides with and helps in drawing a new map of fault lines, self-definitions, and reciprocal definitions with respect to the relationship between the Church, the world, and politics.[27] Pope Francis's pontificate, in how he has presented himself in the first few months and especially in the interview published by the Jesuits, could mean a return to a Catholicism that is in search of "common ground," such as that of the Cardinal of Chicago, Joseph Bernardin (1928–96).[28] America is a crucial place for the pontificate of the "world Church," since it is placed at the intersection of two worlds, between the Christian Europe of the "weak thought" (Gianni Vattimo's *pensiero debole*), and the rest of the world where there is "fierce belief," Gilles Kepel's "revanche de Dieu."[29]

The challenge for Pope Francis is within Catholicism as a "world Church"—the *Weltkirche* of Karl Rahner, and the "world" in general: the Catholic Church, as the political heir of the Roman Empire no less than spiritual daughter of Jesus of Nazareth, requires at the same time ordinary government and extraordinary reforms. The two predecessors of Pope Francis, over the past thirty-five years, had done little of either of these things. The ability of the Catholic Church to govern and reform, under the gaze of the media, who are particularly sympathetic and lenient with Pope Francis, might say something to all those who see the inability of the contemporary world to recover the legitimacy of a foundational ethical-political tradition. With Francis, the papacy abandons the enchanting sirens of the apocalyptic utterances and turns to prophecy.

NOTES

PROLOGUE

1. "After having repeatedly examined my conscience before God, I have come to the certainty that my strengths, due to an advanced age, are no longer suited to an adequate exercise of the Petrine ministry. I am well aware that this ministry, due to its essential spiritual nature, must be carried out not only with words and deeds, but no less with prayer and suffering. However, in today's world, subject to so many rapid changes and shaken by questions of deep relevance for the life of faith, in order to govern the barque of Saint Peter and proclaim the Gospel, both strength of mind and body are necessary, strength which in the last few months, has deteriorated in me to the extent that I have had to recognize my incapacity to adequately fulfill the ministry entrusted to me." The short speech of Benedict XVI to the consistory of February 11, 2013, was given in Latin. For the official English translation, see http://www.vatican.va/holy_father/benedict_xvi/speeches/2013/february/documents/hf_ben-xvi_spe_20130211_declaratio_en.html.

2. Cf. Paul VI's *motu proprio Ingravescentem Aetatem*, November 20, 1970. For the official Latin version, see http://www.vatican.va/holy_father/paul_vi/motu_proprio/documents/hf_p-vi_motu-proprio_19701120_ingravescentem_lt. html. An unoffi-

cial English translation can be found at http:// www.ewtn.com/ library/PAPALDOC/P6INGAET.HTM.

3. Massimo Faggioli, "Il Vaticano II come 'Costituzione' e la 'recezione politica' del concilio," *Rassegna di Teologia* 50 (2009): 107–22.

4. Peter Hünermann, ed., *Exkommunikation oder Kommunikation? Der Weg der Kirche nach dem II. Vatikanum und die Pius-Brüder* (Freiburg: Herder, 2009).

5. Massimo Faggioli, *Il vescovo e il concilio. Modello episcopale e aggiornamento al Vaticano II* (Bologna: Il Mulino, 2005).

6. John W. O'Malley, *What Happened at Vatican II* (Cambridge: Belknap Press of Harvard University Press, 2008).

7. Giuseppe Alberigo, general ed., *History of Vatican II*, 5 vols. (English ed. by Joseph A. Komonchak, Maryknoll, NY: Orbis, 1995–2006).

8. Jean-Marie Tillard, *L'évêque de Rome* (Paris: Cerf 1982); Klaus Schatz, *Der päpstliche Primat. Seine Geschichte von den Ursprüngen bis zur Gegenwart* (Würzburg: Echter, 1990); Emmanuel Lanne, *Tradition et communion des églises. Recueil d'études* (Leuven: Leuven University Press, 1997).

9. John O'Malley, *Tradition in Transition: Historical Perspectives on Vatican II* (Wilmington, DE: M. Glazier, 1989).

10. On John Paul II, various passages in Alberto Melloni, *Chiesa madre, chiesa matrigna* (Turin: Einaudi, 2004); Giovanni Miccoli, *In difesa della fede. La Chiesa di Giovanni Paolo II e Benedetto XVI* (Milan: Rizzoli, 2007); Andrea Riccardi, *Giovanni Paolo II. La biografia* (San Paolo: Cinisello B, 2011).

11. Massimo Faggioli, "Note in margine a recenti contributi per una riforma ecumenica del papato," *Cristianesimo nella Storia* 22, no. 2 (2001): 451–72.

12. Enrico Galavotti, *Processo a Papa Giovanni. La causa di canonizzazione di A. G. Roncalli (1965–2000)* (Bologna: Il Mulino, 2005).

13. Roberto Rusconi, *Santo padre. La santità del papa da San Pietro a Giovanni Paolo II* (Roma: Viella, 2010).

14. Hervé Legrand, "A servizio della chiesa," *Il Regno—attualità* 4 (2013): 107–9.

15. Benedict XVI, address at the audience of February 27, 2013, http://www.vatican.va/holy_father/benedict_xvi/audiences /2013/documents/hf_ben-xvi_aud_20130227_en.html.

16. Rudolf Lill, *Die Macht der Päpste* (Kevelaer: Topos 2006); Thomas Reese, *Inside the Vatican. The Politics and Organization of the Catholic Church* (Cambridge: Harvard University Press, 1996); Andrea Riccardi, *Il potere del papa da Pio XII a Giovanni Paolo II* (Rome-Bari: Laterza, 1993).

17. Alberto Melloni, *L'inizio di papa Ratzinger. Lezioni sul conclave del 2005 e sull'incipit del pontificato di Benedetto XVI* (Turin: Einaudi, 2006).

18. Marcello Neri, "Orfano della modernità," *Il Mulino*, http://www.rivistailmulino.it/news/newsitem/index/Item/News: NEWS_ITEM:2008 (February 12, 2013).

CHAPTER 1

1. Alberto Melloni, *Il conclave. Storia di un'istituzione* (Bologna: Il Mulino, 2005) (new edition updated 2013).

2. Yves Congar, *Le Concile de Vatican II. Son Église, Peuple de Dieu et Corps du Christ* (Paris: Cerf, 1984), 54.

3. Statement by the Secretary of State on February 23, 2013, http://www.news.va/en/news/secretariat-of-state-communique.

4. See http://www.vatican.va/holy_father/benedict_xvi/mo tu_proprio/documents/hf_ben-xvi_motu-proprio_20130222 _normas-nonnullas_en.html. Cf. Kurt Martens, "'*Tu es Petrus, et super hanc petram aedificabo Ecclesiam meam.*' An Analysis of the Legislation for the Vacancy of the Apostolic See and the Election of the Roman Pontiff," *The Jurist* 73, no. 1 (2013): 29–88.

5. See http://www.vatican.va/sede_vacante/2013/homily-pro-eligendo-pontifice_2013_en.html.

6. See http://vaticaninsider.lastampa.it/vaticano/dettaglio-articolo/articolo/conclave-27018/.

7. Alberto Melloni, *L'inizio di papa Ratzinger. Lezioni sul conclave del 2005 e sull'incipit del pontificato di Benedetto XVI* (Turin: Einaudi, 2006), 44–52.

8. Sandro Magister, "Le ultime parole di Bergoglio prima del conclave," http://magister.blogautore.espresso.repubblica.it (March 27, 2013).

9. "L'atlante di papa Francesco," special edition of *Limes* 3 (2013).

10. Gustavo Gutierrez, *A Theology of Liberation: History, Politics, and Salvation,* (Maryknoll NY: Orbis, 1972) (republished several times in several languages, until its forty-year edition in 2012). For the new opening toward the theology of liberation in the Church under Pope Francis, see the book by Gerhard Ludwig Cardinal Müller, *Povera per i poveri. La missione della Chiesa* (Vatican City: Libreria Editrice Vaticana, 2013).

11. On the Argentinian Church and political power, see Loris Zanatta, *Dallo Stato liberale alla nazione cattolica: Chiesa ed esercito nelle origini del peronismo, 1930–1943* (Milan: Franco Angeli, 1996); Roberto Di Stefano and Loris Zanatta, *Historia de la iglesia argentina: desde la conquista hasta fines del siglo XX* (Buenos Aires: Sudamericana, 2009).

12. See http://www.vatican.va/holy_father/francesco/elezione/index_en.htm.

13. See http://www.vatican.va/holy_father/francesco/homilies/2013/documents/papa-francesco_20130314_omelia-cardinali_en.html.

14. See http://www.vatican.va/holy_father/francesco/speeches/2013/march/documents/papa-francesco_20130316_rappresentanti-media_en.html.

15. See http://www.vatican.va/holy_father/francesco/homi

lies/2013/documents/papa-francesco_20130317_omelia-santa-anna_en.html.

16. See http://www.vatican.va/holy_father/francesco/homi lies/2013/documents/papa-francesco_20130319_omelia-inizio-pontificato_en.html.

17. Massimo Faggioli, *True Reform: Liturgy and Ecclesiology in* Sacrosanctum Concilium (Collegeville, MN: Liturgical Press, 2012).

18. Jorge Bergoglio and Abraham Skorka, *Sobre el Cielo y la Tierra* (Buenos Aires: Sudamericana, 2010).

19. See http://www.vatican.va/holy_father/francesco/spee ches/2013/march/documents/papa-francesco_20130320_dele gati-fraterni_en.html.

20. See http://www.vatican.va/holy_father/francesco/homi lies/2013/documents/papa-francesco_20130328_messa-cris male_en.html.

21. See http://www.vatican.va/holy_father/francesco/homi lies/2013/documents/papa-francesco_20130407_omelia-pos sesso-cattedra-laterano_en.html.

22. Massimo Faggioli, "Vatican II and the Church of the Margins," *Theological Studies* 74 (September 2013): 808–18.

23. See http://www.news.va/en/news/pope-francis-appoints -group-of-cardinals-to-advise.

24. See http://www.vatican.va/holy_father/paul_vi/motu_ proprio/documents/hf_p-vi_motu-proprio_19650915_aposto lica-sollicitudo_en.html; Massimo Faggioli, *Il vescovo e il concilio. Modello episcopale e aggiornamento al Vaticano II* (Bologna, Il Mulino, 2008); Antonino Indelicato, *Il sinodo dei vescovi. La collegialità sospesa (1965–1985)* (Bologna: Il Mulino, 2007). Massimo Faggioli, "Reform of the Roman Curia at Vatican II and after Vatican II," *Reform of the Roman Curia*, special issue of *Concilium* 5 (2013): 25–33.

25. Massimo Faggioli, *John XXIII: The Medicine of Mercy* (Collegeville, MN: Liturgical Press, 2014).

26. See Ugo Sartorio's review of the book by Gustavo Gutierrez and Gerhard Ludwig Müller, *Dalla parte dei poveri. Teologia della liberazione, teologia della Chiesa* (Padua-Bologna: Edizioni Messaggero–Editrice Missionaria Italiana, 2013), 192, in *L'Osservatore Romano*, September 4, 2013.

27. "Intervista a Papa Francesco," *La Civiltà Cattolica* 3918 (year 164), September 19, 2013, 449–77, cit. 457–58 (published in various languages throughout the world: in English by *America* under the title "A Big Heart Open to God," September 19, 2013).

28. Paul Vallely, *Pope Francis Untying the Knots* (London: Bloomsury, 2013).

CHAPTER 2

1. Michael D'Antonio has spoken of a "second Porta Pia" after that of 1870, or a "Porta Pia of souls" with regard to the credibility of the Catholic Church, in *Mortal Sins: Sex, Crime, and the Era of Catholic Scandal* (New York: Thomas Dunne Books, 2013).

2. Eliza Griswold, *The Tenth Parallel: Dispatches from the Fault Line between Christianity and Islam* (New York: Picador, 2010).

3. See http://www.vatican.va/holy_father/benedict_xvi/spe eches/2013/february/documents/hf_ben-xvi_spe_20130214 _clero-roma_en.html.

4. Benedict XVI's homily on Ash Wednesday, February 13, 2013, http://www.vatican.va/holy_father/benedict_xvi/homilies/ 2013/documents/hf_ben-xvi_hom_20130213_ceneri_en. html.

5. Andreas Kraus, "Der Kardinal-Nepote Francesco Barberini und das Staatssekretariat Urbans VIII," *Römische Quartalschrift* 64 (1969): 191–208.

6. Ludwig von Pastor, in *Storia dei Papi*, vol. 15 (Rome: Desclée, 1943), 643; cf. Antonio Menniti Ippolito, "Parallele

divergenti? Papa Benedetto XIII e il papato Orsini," *Rivista Storica del Sannio* 15 (2008): 45–66.

7. See Joseph Ratzinger's comment on *Dei Verbum* published in 1967 in *Lexicon für Theologie und Kirche. Das Zweite Vatikanische Konzil*, now republished in two volumes of Joseph Ratzinger-Benedict XVI's writings on the Council: *Joseph Ratzinger—Gesammelte Schriften: Zur Lehre des Zweiten Vatikanischen Konzils: Formulierung—Vermittlung—Deutung* (Bd. 7/1–7/2) (Freiburg: Herder, 2012), 2:715–91.

8. Giuseppe Ruggieri, *La costituzione Anglicanorum coetibus e l'ecumenismo* (Bologna: EDB, 2012).

9. Benedict XVI's speech to the Roman Curia, December 22, 2005, http://www.vatican.va/holy_father/benedict_xvi/spee ches/2005/december/documents/hf_ben_xvi_spe_20051222_roman-curia_en.html.

10. Massimo Faggioli, *Vatican II: The Battle for Meaning* (New York: Paulist Press, 2012).

11. See http://www.vatican.va/holy_father/benedict_xvi/let ters/2007/documents/hf_ben-xvi_let_20070707_lettera-vescovi _en.html; http://www.vatican.va/roman_curia/congregations/ cfaith/documents/rc_con_cfaith_doc_20070629_responsa-quaestiones_en.html.

12. Massimo Faggioli, *True Reform: Liturgy and Ecclesiology in* Sacrosanctum Concilium, (Collegeville, MN: Liturgical Press, 2012).

13. Peter Hünermann, Hrsg., *Exkommunikation oder Kommunikation? Der Weg der Kirche nach dem II. Vatikanum und die Pius-Brüder* (Freiburg: Herder, 2009).

14. Benedict XVI's address to the University of Regensburg, September 12, 2006, http://www.vatican.va/holy_father/bene dict_xvi/speeches/2006/september/documents/hf_ben-xvi_spe_ 20060912_university-regensburg_en.html.

15. Massimo Faggioli, "Vatican II: The History and the 'Narratives,'" *Theological Studies* 73, no. 4 (December 2012):

749–67; Gerald O'Collins, "Does Vatican II Represent Continuity or Discontinuity?" *Theological Studies* 73, no. 4 (December 2012): 768–94; John W. O'Malley, "'The Hermeneutic of Reform': A Historical Analysis," *Theological Studies* 73, no. 3 (September 2012): 517–46; Ormond Rush, "Toward a Comprehensive Interpretation of the Council and Its Documents," *Theological Studies* 73, no. 3 (September 2012): 547–69.

16. See John W. O'Malley, *Trent: What Happened at the Council?* (Cambridge: Belknap Press of Harvard University Press, 2013).

17. Peter Steinfels, *A People Adrift: The Crisis of the Roman Catholic Church in America* (New York: Simon & Schuster, 2003).

18. See Joseph Ratzinger-Benedict XVI, "Discorso alla Curia Romana" (December 22, 2005), in *Insegnamenti di Benedetto XVI* (2005) (Vatican City: Libreria Editrice Vaticana, 2006), 1:1018–32.

19. See Giuseppe Alberigo, ed., *Storia del concilio Vaticano II*, 5 vols., Italian edition by Alberto Melloni (Bologna: Peeters/Il Mulino, 1995–2001) (second edition 2012–14); *History of Vatican II*, vols. 1–5, ed. Giuseppe Alberigo, English version ed. Joseph A. Komonchak (Maryknoll, NY: Orbis, 1995–2006).

20. See *Herders Theologischer Kommentar zum Zweiten Vatikanischen Konzil*, by Hans Jochen Hilberath and Peter Hünermann, 5 vols. (Freiburg: Herder, 2004–5).

21. See Faggioli, *Vatican II: The Battle for Meaning.*

22. See Massimo Faggioli, *Sorting Out Catholicism. Brief History of the New Catholic Movements* (Collegeville, MN: Liturgical Press, 2014).

23. Massimo Faggioli, *Il vescovo e il concilio. Modello episcopale e aggiornamento al Vaticano II* (Bologna: Il Mulino, 2005); Massimo Faggioli, "The Reform of the Roman Curia at Vatican II and After Vatican II," *Concilium* 5 (2013).

24. See James L. Heft and John W. O'Malley, eds., *After Vatican II: Trajectories and Hermeneutics* (Grand Rapids, MI: Eerdmans, 2012).

25. Bergoglio did not fail to express his concern in 2009 in the case of Williamson (who lived in Argentina), as well as in the issue of ordination for Anglicans welcomed by Rome: cf. Paul Vallely, *Pope Francis Untying the Knots* (London: Bloomsury, 2013).

26. See http://www.vatican.va/holy_father/francesco/angel us/2013/documents/papa-francesco_angelus_20130811_en. html.

27. John W. O'Malley, *What Happened at Vatican II?* (Cambridge: Belknap Press of Harvard University Press, 2008).

28. Yves Congar, *Pour une Église servante et pauvre* (Paris: Cerf, 1963).

29. Christoph Theobald, *Le Christianisme comme style. Une manière de faire de la théologie en post-modernité* (Paris: Cerf, 2007).

30. Declaration on the occasion of the twenty-fifth anniversary of the episcopal consecrations [by Archbishop Marcel Lefebvre, of June 30, 1988], dated June 27, 2013, and signed by three Lefebvrian bishops Bernard Fellay, Bernard Tissier de Mallerais, and Alfonso de Gallareta in http://www.dici.org/en/ documents/dichiarazione-nella-ricorrenza-del-25-anniversario- delle-consacrazioni-episcopali-30-giugno-1988-27-giugno- 2013/, par. 3.

31. See Benedict XVI's Address to the Roman Curia, December 22, 2005, http://www.vatican.va/holy_father/bene dict_xvi/speeches/2005/december/documents/hf_ben_xvi_spe_2 0051222_roman-curia_en.html.

CHAPTER 3

1. José Casanova, *Public Religions in the Modern World* (Chicago: University of Chicago Press, 1994).

2. Yves Congar, "Le siècle de l'Église," in *L'Église de saint Augustin à l'époque moderne* (Paris: Cerf, 1970), 459–77.

3. Brad Gregory, *The Unintended Reformation: How a Religious Revolution Secularized Society* (Cambridge: Harvard University Press, 2012).

4. Charles Taylor, *A Secular Age* (Cambridge: Harvard University Press, 2007).

5. Giorgio Agamben, *Il mistero del male. Benedetto XVI e la fine dei tempi* (Rome-Bari: Laterza, 2013).

6. See Severino Dianich, "La Chiesa dopo la Chiesa," *Il Regno—attualità* 14 (2013): 463–75.

7. "The Church Becomes a State, the State Becomes a Church," in Francis Fukuyama's, *The Origins of Political Order: From Prehuman Times to the French Revolution* (New York: Farrar, Strauss and Giroux, 2012), 262–89—which revisits Harold Berman, *Law and Revolution: The Formation of the Western Legal Tradition* (Cambridge: Harvard University Press, 1983).

8. "Successor of the Prince of the Apostles, Supreme Pontiff of the Universal Church, Primate of Italy, Archbishop and Metropolitan bishop of the Roman Province, Sovereign of the State of Vatican City, Servant of the Servants of God." On page one of the Pontifical Yearbook, the Roman see is presented first: in the 2013, Benedict XVI is referred to as "the supreme pontiff emeritus."

9. Antonio Spadaro, *Cyberteologia. Pensare il cristianesimo al tempo della rete* (Milan: Vita & Pensiero, 2012; English trans. New York: Fordham University Press, 2014); Federico Ruozzi, *Il Concilio in diretta. Il Vaticano II e la televisione tra informazione e partecipazione* (Bologna: Il Mulino, 2012).

10. Andrea Riccardi, *Governo carismatico. 25 anni di pontificato* (Milan: Mondadori, 2003).

11. José Casanova, "Nuovi movimenti religiosi: Fenomeno globale. Secolarizzazione, risveglio religioso, fondamentalismo." *Il Regno—attualità* 10 (May 15, 2013): 317–29.

12. George Weigel, *Evangelical Catholicism: Deep Reform in the 21st-Century Church* (New York: Basic Books, 2013). On Michael Novak, see his interesting autobiography, *Writing from Left to Right: My Journey from Liberal to Conservative* (New York: Image, 2013).

13. The transcription of the interview on July 28, 2013: http://www.vatican.va/holy_father/francesco/speeches/2013/july /documents/papa-francesco_20130728_gmg-conferenza-stampa_en.html.

14. Gianfranco Brunelli, "L'enciclica di Rio," *Il Regno—attualità* 14 (2013): 409–10.

15. Antonio Spadaro, SJ, "Intervista a Papa Francesco," *La Civiltà Cattolica* 3918 (year 164), September 19, 2013, 449–77 (simultaneously published in different languages in sixteen different Jesuit magazines throughout the world, and in English in *America* under the title "A Big Heart Open to God," September 19, 2013).

16. See the classic study by Walter Ullmann, *The Growth of Papal Government in the Middle Ages: A Study in the Ideological Relation of Clerical to Lay Power* (Cambridge, UK: Methuen, 1955), 147.

17. Ormond Rush, "Ecclesial Conversion after Vatican II: Forever Becoming a Church That Reveals the 'Genuine Face of God,'" a paper delivered at the convention of the Catholic Theological Society of America (Miami, June 8, 2013). See also Peter De Mey, "Church Renewal and Reform in the Documents of Vatican II: History, Theology, Terminology," *The Jurist* 71 (2011): 360–400; and John W. O'Malley, "'The Hermeneutic of Reform': A Historical Analysis," *Theological Studies* 73 (2012): 517–46.

18. Avery Dulles, "The Church Always in Need of Reform: *Ecclesia Semper Reformanda*," in *The Church Inside and Out* (Washington, DC: United States Catholic Conference, 1974), 37–50.

19. Francis Fukuyama, *The End of History and the Last Man* (New York: Avon, 1992), (expanding an article published in the

fateful year 1989: Francis Fukuyama, "The End of History?" *The National Interest* 16 [1989]: 3–18).

20. Paolo Prodi, *Il paradigma tridentino. Un'epoca della storia della Chiesa* (Brescia: Morcelliana, 2010).

21. Lieven Boeve, "Une histoire de changement et conflit des paradigms théologiques? Vatican II et sa réception entre continuité et discontinuité," in *La théologie catholique entre intransigeance et renouveau*, eds. Gilles Routhier, Philippe J. Roy, Karim Schelkens (Louvain-la-Neuve: Collège Érasme, 2011), 355–66.

22. Constitution on the Liturgy *Sacrosanctum Concilium*, no. 1: cf. Massimo Faggioli, *True Reform: Liturgy and Ecclesiology in Sacrosanctum Concilium* (Collegeville, MN: Liturgical Press, 2012).

23. Ormond Rush, *Still Interpreting Vatican II: Some Hermeneutical Principles* (New York/Mahwah, NJ: Paulist Press, 2004), 69–85, cit. 78.

24. Karl Rahner, "Basic Theological Interpretation of the Second Vatican Council," in *Concern for the Church* (New York: Crossroad, 1981), 77–90, cit. 83.

25. Christoph Theobald, *La réception du concile Vatican II. I. Accéder à la source* (Paris: Cerf, 2009), 409.

26. Massimo Faggioli, "Post-fazione. Il Vaticano II come spartiacque nel dibattito su donne e teologia," in *"Tantum aurora est". Donne e concilio Vaticano II*, eds. Marinella Perroni, Alberto Melloni, and Serena Noceti (Berlin: LIT, 2012), 353–68; Massimo Faggioli, "Concili: tra testi e contesti," in *Avendo qualcosa da dire. Teologi e teologhe rileggono il Vaticano II*, eds. Marinella Perroni and Hervé Legrand (Milan: San Paolo, 2014), 75–83.

27. See the account of the meeting between the pope and the president of the CLAR (Latin American Confederation of Religious) on June 6, 2013; cf. Lorenzo Prezzi, "Spazio alle alternative," *Il Regno—attualità* 14 (2013): 423–25.

28. See the SSPX's Bishops' declaration for the 25th anniversary (delivered to Archbishop. Marcel Lefebvre, on June 30, 1988),

dated June 27, 2013, and signed by three Lefebvrian bishops: Bernard Fellay, Bernard Tissier de Mallerais, and Alfonso de Gallareta, at http://sspx.org/en/sspxs-bishops-declaration-25th-anniversary.

29. Hermann J. Pottmeyer, *Towards a Papacy in Communion: Perspectives from Vatican Councils I & II* (New York: Crossroad, 1998), 110.

30. John R. Quinn, *The Reform of the Papacy* (New York: Crossroad, 1999) and by the same author, *Ever Ancient, Ever New: Structures of Communion in the Church* (New York/Mahwah, NJ: Paulist Press, 2013).

31. See the table of contents of the volume *The Roman Curia and the Communion of Churches*, eds. Peter Huizing and Knut Walf, *Concilium* 127, no. 7 (1979).

32. Peter Hünermann, "Kirchliche Vermessung Lateinamerikas. Theologische Reflexionen aus der Dokument von Aparecida," *Theologische Quartalschrift* 188 (2008): 15–30.

33. Massimo Faggioli, *Breve storia dei movimenti cattolici* (Rome: Carocci, 2008) (Spanish trans. Madrid: PPC, 2011; English trans. Collegeville: Liturgical Press, 2014); Massimo Faggioli, *Nello spirito del concilio. Movimenti ecclesiali e recezione del Vaticano II* (Milan: Edizioni San Paolo, 2013).

34. See the pope's speech to the papal representatives of June 21, 2013, http://www.vatican.va/holy_father/francesco/speeches/2013/june/documents/papa-francesco_20130621_rappresent anti-pontifici_en.html.

35. See http://www.news.va/it/news/il-papa-costituisce-un-gruppo-di-cardinali-per-la.

36. René Laurentin, "Paul VI et l'après-concile," in *Paul VI et la modernité dans l'Église* (Rome: École Française de Rome, 1984), 575.

37. Speech of Pope Francis to the Brazilian episcopate, July 27, 2013, http://www.vatican.va/holy_father/francesco/speeches

/2013/july/documents/papa-francesco_20130727_gmg-episco pato-brasile_en.html.

38. Among the ideologizations, Pope Francis enumerated "social reductionism, psychological ideologization, the Gnostic proposal, and the Pelagian proposal": Pope Francis's speech to the bishops in charge of the Latin American Episcopal Council (CELAM), July 28, 2013, http://www.vatican.va/holy_father/ francesco/speeches/2013/july/documents/papa-francesco_ 20130728_gmg-celam-rio_en.html.

39. See http://www.vatican.va/holy_father/francesco/spee ches/2014/february/documents/papa-francesco_20140227_riun ione-congregazione-vescovi_en.html.

EPILOGUE

1. Karl Rahner, "Basic Theological Interpretation of the Second Vatican Council," in *Concern for the Church* (New York: Crossroad, 1981), 77–90.

2. Marcello Neri, "Passione per l'umano," *Il Mulino rivista online*, http://www.rivistailmulino.it/news/newsitem/index/Item /News:NEWS_ITEM:2290, August 7, 2013.

3. Samuel P. Huntington, *The Third Wave: Democratization in the Late Twentieth Century* (Norman, OK: University of Oklahoma Press, 1991); Philippe Chenaux, *Une Europe vaticane? Entre le plan Marshall et les traités de Rome* (Brussells: Ciaco, 1990); Philippe Chenaux, *L'Église catholique et le communisme en Europe (1917–1989). De Lénine à Jean-Paul II* (Paris: Cerf, 2009).

4. See "*L'impero del Papa*," special edition of the Italian journal of geopolitics *Limes* 1 (2000).

5. See Paul Vallely, *Pope Francis Untying the Knots* (London: Bloomsury, 2013).

6. Wolfram Kaiser, *Christian Democracy and the Origins of*

European Union (Cambridge, UK: Cambridge University Press, 2011), 163–90.

7. See the homilies and speeches by Pope Francis in two "margins" of Italy, on the island of Lampedusa on July 8, 2013, at http://www.vatican.va/holy_father/francesco/speeches/2013/sept ember/documents/papa-francesco_20130922_lavoratori-cag liari_en.html.

8. See the speech to the representatives of the World Meeting of Popular Movements (October 28, 2014), in http://w2. vatican.va/content/francesco/it/speeches/2014/october/docu ments/papa-francesco_20141028_incontro-mondiale-movi menti-popolari.html.

9. The text of Francis's speech of October 4, 2014, at http://w2.vatican.va/content/francesco/en/speeches/2014/octo ber/documents/papa-francesco_20141004_incontro-per-la-famiglia.html.

10. For the relationship between Joseph Ratzinger and *Gaudium et Spes,* see Joseph Ratzinger, "A Review of Post-Conciliar Era," in *Principles of Catholic Theology* (San Francisco: Ignatius Press, 1987), 367–93.

11. Pope Francis, letter to Cardinal Lorenzo Baldisseri, secretary general of the Bishop's Synod, April 1, 2014, in http://w2. vatican.va/content/francesco/it/letters/2014/documents/papa-francesco_20140401_cardinale-baldisseri.html.

12. See Marie-Dominique Chenu, *La doctrine social de l'église comme idéologie* (Paris: Cerf, 1979).

13. "The temptation to greed is ever present. We encounter it also in the great prophecy of Ezekiel on the shepherds, which Saint Augustine commented upon in one his celebrated sermons which we have just reread in the Liturgy of the Hours. Greed for money and power. And to satisfy this greed, evil pastors lay intolerable burdens on the shoulders of others, which they themselves do not lift a finger to move." The text of Pope Francis's homily on October 5, 2014, in http://w2.vatican.va/content/francesco/en/

homilies/2014/documents/papa-francesco_20141005_omelia-apertura-sinodo-vescovi.html.

14. For an authoritative interpretation of the Synod of 2014 from one of the closest confidants of Pope Francis and member of the Synod, see Antonio Spadaro, SJ, "Una chiesa in cammino sinodale. Le sfide pastorali sulla famiglia," *Civiltà Cattolica* 3945 (November 1, 2014): 213–27.

15. See *Evangelii Gaudium* (November 24, 2013), par. 223: "Giving priority to space means madly attempting to keep everything together in the present, trying to possess all the spaces of power and of self-assertion; it is to crystallize processes and presume to hold them back. Giving priority to time means being concerned about initiating processes rather than possessing spaces. Time governs spaces, illumines them and makes them links in a constantly expanding chain, with no possibility of return."

16. See Andrea Riccardi, *Il potere del papa. Da Pio XII a Giovanni Paolo II* (Roma-Bari: Laterza, 1993).

17. For a typical American Catholic conservative reaction to the Synod of October 2014 and more generally to Pope Francis, see Ross Douthat, "The Pope and the Precipice," *New York Times*, October 25, 2014. See also the nuanced but firm reply by John W. O'Malley, "Is a Precipice Yawning?" *America*, October 29, 2014, http://americamagazine.org/content/all-things/precipice-yawning-john-w-omalley-sj-responds-ross-douthat.

18. For the differences between "social" Catholicism and "liberal" Catholicism in America, see John McGreevy, *Catholicism and American Freedom: A History* (New York: W. W. Norton, 2004).

19. In the case of Argentina, see Loris Zanatta, *Dallo Stato liberale alla nazione cattolica: Chiesa ed esercito nelle origini del peronismo, 1930–1943* (Milan: Franco Angeli, 1996); Roberto Di Stefano and Loris Zanatta, *Historia de la iglesia argentina: desde la conquista hasta fines del siglo XX* (Buenos Aires: Sudamericana, 2009).

20. Paul Gauthier, *La chiesa dei poveri e il concilio* (Florence: Vallecchi, 1965).

21. Peter Steinfels, *A People Adrift: The Crisis of the Roman Catholic Church in America* (New York: Simon & Schuster, 2003); Massimo Faggioli, "Vatican II: The History and the 'Narratives,'" *Theological Studies* 73, no. 4 (December 2012): 749–67.

22. One example would be Giuliano Ferrara's article, "La sposa infedele," *Il Foglio*, September 21, 2013.

23. David Gibson, "Pope Francis Is Unsettling—and Dividing—the Catholic Right," *National Catholic Reporter*, August 8, 2013, http://ncronline.org/news/vatican/pope-francis-unsettling-and-dividing-catholic-right. See in particular the interview with the Archbishop of Philadelphia, Archbishop Chaput, July 23, 2013, http://ncronline.org/blogs/ncr-today/right-wing-generally-not-happy-francis-chaput-says.

24. Michael D'Antonio, "More Catholic than the Pope," *Foreign Policy*, July 30, 2013, http://www.foreignpolicy.com/articles/2013/07/30/more_catholic_than_the_pope_francis_homosexuality_reform.

25. Pierangelo Sequeri, *L'amore della ragione. Variazioni sinfoniche su un tema di Benedetto XVI* (Bologna: EDB, 2012), 90.

26. Paul Baumann, "Rome's Cassandra: On George Weigel," *The Nation*, June 3, 2013.

27. See the debate between *America* and *Commonweal* a few weeks after Pope Francis's election: Matt Malone, SJ, "Pursuing the Truth in Love: The Mission of *America* in a 21st-Century Church," *America*, June 3–10, 2013, and "*America*'s Politics," editorial of *Commonweal*, August 29, 2013.

28. *Catholic Common Ground Initiative: Foundational Documents* (Eugene, OR: Wipf and Stock, 2002).

29. See Sequeri, *L'amore della ragione*, 112.

BIBLIOGRAPHY

Agamben, Giorgio. *Il mistero del male: Benedetto XVI e la fine dei tempi.* Rome-Bari: Laterza, 2013.

Alberigo, Giuseppe, general editor. *History of Vatican II.* 5 vols. English edition by Jospeh A. Komonchak. Maryknoll, NY: Orbis, 1995–2006.

Allen, John L., Jr. *The Future Church: How Ten Trends Are Revolutionizing the Catholic Church.* New York: Doubleday, 2009.

"L'atlante di papa Francesco," in *Limes: Rivista italiana di geopolitica* 3, 2013.

Faggioli, Massimo. *Vatican II: The Battle for Meaning.* New York / Mahwah, NJ: Paulist Press, 2012.

Hünermann, Peter, ed. *Exkommunikation oder Kommunikation? Der Weg der Kirche nach dem II. Vatikanum und die Pius-Brüder.* Freiburg: Herder, 2009.

Lill, Rudolf. *Die Macht der Päpste.* Kevelaer: Topos, 2006.

Massa, Mark. *Catholics and American Culture. Fulton Sheen, Dorothy Day, and the Notre Dame Football Team.* New York: Crossroad, 1999.

McGreevy, John. *Catholicism and American Freedom: A History.* New York: W. W. Norton, 2004.

Melloni, Alberto. *Il conclave. Storia di un'istituzione.* Bologna: Il Mulino, 2005 (new edition, 2013).

———. *L'inizio di papa Ratzinger. Lezioni sul conclave del 2005 e sull'incipit del pontificato di Benedetto XVI.* Turin: Einaudi, 2006.

O'Malley, John W. *What Happened at Vatican II*. Cambridge: Belknap Press of Harvard University Press, 2008.

Reese, Thomas J. *Inside the Vatican: The Politics and Organization of the Catholic Church*. Cambridge: Harvard University Press, 1996.

Riccardi, Andrea. *Il potere del papa da Pio XII a Giovanni Paolo II*. Rome-Bari: Laterza, 1993.

Rubin, Sergio, and Francesca Ambrogetti. *El Jesuita. Conversaciones con el cardinal Jorge Bergoglio, sj*. Buenos Aires: Vergara—Grupo Zeta, 2010.

Ruggieri, Giuseppe. *La verità crocifissa. Il pensiero cristiano di fronte all'alterità*. Rome: Carocci, 2007.

Scatena, Silvia. *La teologia della liberazione in America Latina*. Rome: Carocci, 2008.

Sequeri, Pierangelo. *L'amore della ragione. Variazioni sinfoniche su un tema di Benedetto XVI*. Bologna: EDB, 2012.

Spadaro, Antonio. *Il disegno di papa Francesco. Il volto futuro della Chiesa*. Bologna: EMI, 2013.

———. "Intervista a papa Francesco," *Civilta Cattolica* 3918 (September 19, 2013), 449–77. English translation: *A Big Heart Open to God: A Conversation with Pope Francis*. Introduction by Matt Malone, SJ, and spiritual reflection by James Martin, SJ. New York: HarperOne, 2013.

Steinfels, Peter. *A People Adrift: The Crisis of the Roman Catholic Church in America*. New York: Simon & Schuster, 2003.

Vallely, Paul. *Pope Francis Untying the Knots*. London: Bloomsury, 2013.

Verweyen, Hansjürgen. *Joseph Ratzinger-Benedikt XVI: Die Entwicklung seines Denkens*. Darmstadt: Primus, 2007.